Collins

GW00649783

Pocket

English

Grammar

HarperCollins Publishers
Westerhill Road
Bishopbriggs
Glasgow
G64 2QT

First Edition 2012

Previously published as
Collins COBUILD Active
English Grammar

Reprint 10 9 8 7 6 5 4 3 2 1 0

© HarperCollins Publishers
2003, 2012

ISBN 978-0-00-744326-0

Collins® and COBUILD® are
registered trademarks of
HarperCollins Publishers Limited

www.collinslanguage.com

A catalogue record for this book
is available from the British
Library

Typeset by Davidson Publishing
Solutions, Glasgow

Printed and bound in China by
South China Printing Co. Ltd

Acknowledgements
We would like to thank those
authors and publishers who
kindly gave permission for
copyright material to be used in
the Collins Corpus. We would
also like to thank Times
Newspapers Ltd for providing
valuable data.

Editorial Consultant
Penny Hands

Senior Editor
Kate Wild

For the publisher
Lucy Cooper
Kerry Ferguson
Elaine Higgleton
Lisa Sutherland

We would like to thank the
following for their contributions
to previous editions:
Maree Airlie, Michela Clari,
Gwyneth Fox, Lorna Sinclair
Knight, Ramesh Krishnamurthy,
Alison Macaulay,
Christina Rammell,
Keith Stuart, Jenny Watson

CONTENTS

INTRODUCTION

The **Collins COBUILD Pocket English Grammar** provides learners of English from intermediate level upwards with the grammar they need to know for effective use of English. The most important points of English grammar are explained in a clear, simple way, with hundreds of examples showing grammatical structures in use. The examples have been taken from the Collins Corpus, a collection of contemporary texts from different sources, totalling over 4.5 billion words. The units have been logically organized and there are numerous notes to warn of potential errors. In addition, there is a supplement containing practical information about the use of grammar in academic and business contexts and a glossary that gives full explanations of all the specialist terminology.

The attractive colour layout and spacious design makes the **Collins COBUILD Pocket English Grammar** user-friendly and easily accessible – the ideal reference tool for learners of English.

LIST OF UNITS

PRONOUNS AND POSSESSIVES

DETERMINERS

ADJECTIVES

COMPARISON

ADVERBIALS

PREPOSITIONS

TYPES OF VERB

TENSES AND VERB FORMS

CONDITIONALS AND HYPOTHETICAL SITUATIONS

-ING CLAUSES AND INFINITIVES

DIRECT AND REPORTED SPEECH

THE PASSIVE

MODALS

RELATIVE CLAUSES AND PARTICIPLE CLAUSES

OTHER KINDS OF CLAUSE

Unit 1: Clauses and sentences

Main points

- Simple sentences have one clause.
- Clauses usually consist of a noun phrase as the subject, and a verb phrase.
- Clauses can also have another noun phrase as the object or complement.
- Clauses can have an adverbial, also called an adjunct.
- Changing the order of the words in a clause can change its meaning.
- Compound sentences consist of two or more main clauses. Complex sentences always include a subordinate clause, as well as one or more main clauses.

1 A simple sentence has one clause, beginning with a noun phrase called the subject. The subject is the person or thing that the sentence is about. This is followed by a verb phrase, which tells you what the subject is doing, or describes the subject's situation.

> *I waited.*
> *The girl screamed.*

2 The verb phrase may be followed by another noun phrase, which is called the object. The object is the person or thing affected by the action or situation.

> *He opened <u>the car door</u>.*
> *She married <u>a young engineer</u>.*

After linking verbs like 'be', 'become', 'feel', and 'seem', the verb phrase may be followed by a noun phrase or an adjective, called a complement. The complement tells you more about the subject.

> *She is <u>a doctor</u>.*
> *He seemed <u>angry</u>.*

3 The verb phrase, the object, or the complement can be followed by an adverb or a prepositional phrase, called an adverbial. The adverbial tells you more about the action or situation, for example how, when, or where it happens. Adverbials are also called adjuncts.

> *They shouted <u>loudly</u>.*
> *She won the competition <u>last week</u>.*
> *He was a policeman <u>in Birmingham</u>.*

4 The word order of a clause is different when the clause is a statement, a question, or a command.

> <u>*He speaks*</u> *English very well.* (statement)

Did she win at the Olympics? (question)
Stop her. (command)

Note that the subject is omitted in commands, so the verb comes first.

---

5 A compound sentence has two or more main clauses: that is, clauses which are equally important. You usually join them with 'and', 'but', or 'or'.

He met Jane at the station _and_ went shopping.
I wanted to go _but_ I felt too ill.
You can come now _or_ you can meet us there later.

Note that the order of the two clauses can change the meaning of the sentence.

He went shopping _and_ met Jane at the station.

If the subject of both clauses is the same, you usually omit the subject in the second clause.

I wanted to go _but felt_ too ill.

---

6 A complex sentence contains a subordinate clause and at least one main clause. A subordinate clause gives information about a main clause, and is introduced by a conjunction such as

'because', 'if', 'that', or a 'wh'-word.
Subordinate clauses can come before,
after, or inside the main clause.

> _When he stopped_, no one said anything.

> _If you want_, I'll teach you.

> They were going by car _because it was more comfortable_.

> I told him _that nothing was going to happen to me_.

> The car _that I drove_ was a Ford.

> The man _who came into the room_ was small.

Unit 2: The noun phrase

Main points

- Noun phrases can be the subject, object, or complement of a verb, or the object of a preposition.
- Noun phrases can be nouns on their own, but often include other words such as determiners, numbers, and adjectives.
- Noun phrases can also be pronouns.
- Singular noun phrases take singular verbs; plural noun phrases take plural verbs.

1 Noun phrases are used to say which people or things you are talking about. They can be the subject or object of a verb.

> _Strawberries_ are very expensive now.
> Keith likes _strawberries_.

A noun phrase can also be the complement of a linking verb such as 'be', 'become', 'feel', or 'seem'.

> She became _champion_ in 1964.
> He seemed _a nice man_.

A noun phrase can be used after a preposition, and is often called the object

14

of the preposition.

> I saw him in <u>town</u>.
> She was very ill for <u>six months</u>.

---

2 A noun phrase can be a noun on its own, but it often includes other words. A noun phrase can have a determiner such as 'the' or 'a'. You put determiners at the beginning of the noun phrase.

> <u>The girls</u> were not in <u>the house</u>.
> He was eating <u>an apple</u>.

---

3 A noun phrase can include an adjective. You usually put the adjective in front of the noun.

> He was using <u>blue ink</u>.
> I like living in <u>a big city</u>.

Sometimes you can use another noun in front of the noun.

> I like <u>chocolate cake</u>.
> She wanted a job in <u>the oil industry</u>.

A noun with 's (apostrophe s) is used in front of another noun to show who or what something belongs to or is connected with.

> I held <u>Sheila's hand</u> very tightly.
> He pressed a button on <u>the ship's radio</u>.

4 A noun phrase can also have an adverbial, a relative clause, or a 'to'-infinitive clause after it, which makes it more precise.

> I spoke to _a girl in a dark grey dress_.
> She wrote to _the man who employed me_.
> I was trying to think of _a way to stop him_.

A common adverbial used after a noun is a prepositional phrase beginning with 'of'.

> He tied the rope to _a large block of stone_.
> _The front door of the house_ was wide open.
> I hated _the idea of leaving him alone_.

Participles and some adjectives can also be used after a noun.
→ See Units 36 and 102.

> She pointed to _the three cards lying on the table_.
> He is _the only man available_.

5 Numbers come after determiners and before adjectives.

> I had to pay _a thousand dollars_.
> _Three tall men_ came out of the shed.

6 A noun phrase can also be a pronoun. You often use a pronoun when you are referring back to a person or thing that you have already mentioned.

I've got two boys, and they both enjoy
playing football.

You also use a pronoun when you do not
know who the person or thing is, or do
not want to be precise.

Someone is coming to mend it tomorrow.

---

7 A noun phrase can refer to one or more
people or things. Many nouns have a
singular form referring to one person or
thing, and a plural form referring to more
than one person or thing.
→ See Unit 14.

My car has broken down.
They have two cars.

Similarly, different pronouns are used in
the singular and in the plural.

I am going home now.
We want more money.

When a singular noun phrase is the
subject, it takes a singular verb. When a
plural noun phrase is the subject, it takes
a plural verb.

His son plays football for the school.
Her letters are always very short.

Unit 3: The verb phrase

Main points

- In a clause, the verb phrase usually comes after the subject and always has a main verb.
- The main verb has several different forms.
- Verb phrases can also include one or two auxiliaries, or a modal, or a modal and one or two auxiliaries.
- The verb phrase changes in negative clauses and questions.
- Some verb phrases are followed by an adverbial, a complement, an object, or two objects.

1 The verb phrase in a clause is used to say what is happening in an action or situation. You usually put the verb phrase immediately after the subject. The verb phrase always includes a main verb.

   I _waited_.
   He _bought_ a new car.

---

2 Regular verbs have four forms: the base form, the third person singular form of the

present simple, the '-ing' participle, and the '-ed' form used for the past simple and for the '-ed' participle.

ask	asks	asking	asked
dance	dances	dancing	danced
reach	reaches	reaching	reached
try	tries	trying	tried
dip	dips	dipping	dipped

Irregular verbs may have three forms, four forms, or five forms.

Note that 'be' has eight forms.

cost	costs	costing		
think	thinks	thinking	thought	
swim	swims	swimming	swam	swum
be	am/is/are	being	was/were	been

See pages 474–479 for details of verb forms.

3 The main verb can have one or two auxiliaries in front of it.

   I _had met_ him before.
   The car _was being repaired_.

The main verb can have a modal in front of it.

   You _can go_ now.
   I _would like_ to ask you a question.

The main verb can have a modal and one or two auxiliaries in front of it.

> I _could have spent_ the whole year on it.
> She _would have been delighted_ to see you.

---

4 In negative clauses, you have to use a modal or auxiliary and put 'not' after the first word of the verb phrase.

> He _does not speak_ English very well.
> I _was not smiling_.
> It _could not have been_ wrong.

Note that you often use short forms rather than 'not'.

> I _didn't_ know that.
> He _couldn't_ see it.

---

5 In 'yes/no' questions, you have to put an auxiliary or modal first, then the subject, then the rest of the verb phrase.

> _Did_ you _meet_ George?
> _Couldn't_ you _have been_ a bit quieter?

In 'wh'-questions, you put the 'wh'-word first. If the 'wh'-word is the subject, you put the verb phrase next.

> Which _came_ first?
> Who _could have done_ it?

If the 'wh'-word is the object or an adverbial, you must use an auxiliary or modal next, then the subject, then the rest of the verb phrase.

> What <u>did</u> you <u>do</u>?
> Where <u>could</u> she <u>be going</u>?

---

6 Some verb phrases have an object or two objects after them.
→ See Units 58 and 59.

> He closed <u>the door</u>.
> She sends <u>you her love</u>.

Verb phrases involving linking verbs, such as 'be', have a complement after them.
→ See Unit 62.

> They were <u>sailors</u>.
> She felt <u>happy</u>.

Some verb phrases have an adverbial after them.

> We walked <u>through the park</u>.
> She put the letter <u>on the table</u>.

Unit 4: The imperative and 'let'

Main points

- The imperative is the same as the base form of a verb.
- You form a negative imperative with 'do not', 'don't', or 'never'.
- You use the imperative to ask or tell someone to do something, or to give advice, warnings, or instructions on how to do something.
- You use 'let' when you are offering to do something, making suggestions, or telling someone to do something.

1 The imperative is the same as the base form of a verb. You do not use a pronoun in front of it.

> _Come_ to my place.
> _Start_ when you hear the bell.

2 You form a negative imperative by putting 'do not', 'don't', or 'never' in front of the verb.

> _Do not write_ in this book.

Don't go so fast.
Never open the front door to strangers.

---

3 You use the imperative when you are:

- asking or telling someone to do something

  Pass the salt.
  Hurry up!

- giving someone advice or a warning

  Mind your head.
  Take care!

- giving someone instructions on how to do something

  Put this bit over here, so it fits into that hole.
  Turn right off Broadway into Caxton Street.

---

4 When you want to make an imperative more polite or more emphatic, you can put 'do' in front of it.

  Do have a chocolate biscuit.
  Do stop crying.
  Do be careful.

---

5 The imperative is also used in written instructions on how to do something, for example on notices and packets of food, and in books.

If there is an emergency, <u>dial</u> 999.
<u>Store</u> in a dry place.
<u>Fry</u> the chopped onion and pepper in the oil.

Note that written instructions usually have to be short. This means that words such as 'the' are often omitted.

Wear rubber gloves.
Turn off switch.
Wipe bulb.

Written imperatives are also used to give warnings.

<u>Reduce</u> speed now.

---

6 You use 'let me' followed by the base form of a verb when you are offering to do something for someone.

<u>Let me</u> take your coat.
<u>Let me</u> give you a few details.

---

7 You use 'let's' followed by the base form of a verb when you are suggesting what you and someone else should do.

<u>Let's go</u> outside.
<u>Let's look</u> at our map.

Note that the form 'let us' is only used in formal English.

<u>Let us</u> consider a very simple example.

You put 'do' before 'let's' when you are very keen to do something.

> *Do let's get a taxi.*

The negative of 'let's' is 'let's not' or 'don't let's'.

> *Let's not talk about that.*
> *Don't let's actually write it in the book.*

---

8 You use 'let' followed by a noun phrase and the base form of a verb when you are telling someone to do something or to allow someone else to do it.

> *Let me see it.*
> *Let Philip have a look at it.*

Unit 5: Questions

Main points

- In most questions the first verb comes before the subject.
- 'Yes/no'-questions begin with an auxiliary or a modal.
- 'Wh'-questions begin with a 'wh'-word.

1 Questions which can be answered 'yes' or 'no' are called 'yes/no'-questions.

> *'Are you ready?'* – *'Yes.'*
> *'Have you read this magazine?'* – *'No.'*

If the verb phrase has more than one word, the first word comes at the beginning of the sentence, before the subject. The rest of the verb phrase comes after the subject.

> <u>*Is he*</u> *coming?*
> <u>*Can John*</u> *swim?*
> <u>*Will you*</u> *have finished by lunchtime?*
> <u>*Couldn't you*</u> *have been a bit quieter?*
> <u>*Has he*</u> *been working?*

2 If the verb phrase consists of only a main verb, you use the auxiliary 'do', 'does', or 'did' at the beginning of the sentence, before the subject. After the subject you use the base form of the verb.

Do the British take sport seriously?
Does that sound like anyone you know?
Did Mark call?

Note that when the main verb is 'do', you still have to add 'do', 'does', or 'did' before the subject.

Do they do the work themselves?
Did you do the dishes?

---

3 If the main verb is 'have', you usually put 'do', 'does', or 'did' before the subject.

Does anyone have a question?
Did you have a good flight?

When 'have' means 'own' or 'possess', you can put it before the subject, without using 'do', 'does', or 'did', but this is less common.

Has he any idea what it's like?

---

4 If the main verb is the present simple or past simple of 'be', you put the verb at the beginning of the sentence, before the subject.

Are you ready?
Was it lonely without us?

5 When you want someone to give you more information than just 'yes' or 'no', you ask a 'wh'-question, which begins with a 'wh'-word:

what	when	where	which	who
whom	whose	why	how	

Note that 'whom' is only used in formal English.

6 When a 'wh'-word is the subject of a question, the 'wh'-word comes first, then the verb phrase. You do not add 'do', 'does', or 'did' as an auxiliary.

> <u>*What*</u> *happened?*
> <u>*Which*</u> *is the best restaurant?*
> <u>*Who*</u> *could have done it?*

7 When a 'wh'-word is the object of a verb or preposition, the 'wh'-word comes first, then you follow the rules for 'yes/no'-questions, adding 'do', 'does', or 'did' where necessary.

> <u>*How many*</u> *are there?*
> <u>*Which*</u> *do you like best?*

If there is a preposition, it comes at the end. However, you always put the preposition before 'whom'.

> <u>*What's*</u> *this <u>for</u>?*

With whom were you talking?

Note that you follow the same rules as for 'wh'-words as objects when the question begins with 'when', 'where', 'why', or 'how'.

When will you arrive?
Why did you do it?
Where did you get that *from*?

---

8 You can also use 'what', 'which', 'whose', 'how many', and 'how much' with a noun.

Whose idea was it?
How much money have we got in the bank?

You can use 'which', 'how many', and 'how much' with 'of' and a noun phrase.

Which of the suggested answers was the correct one?
How many of them came?

→ See Unit 6 for more information on 'wh'-words.

Unit 6: 'Wh'- questions

Main points

- You use 'who', 'whom', and 'whose' to ask about people, and 'which' to ask about people or things.
- You use 'what' to ask about things, and 'what for' to ask about reasons and purposes.
- You use 'how' to ask about the way something happens.
- You use 'when' to ask about times, 'why' to ask about reasons, and 'where' to ask about places and directions.

1 You use 'who', 'whom', or 'whose' in questions about people. 'Who' is used to ask questions about the subject or object of the verb, or about the object of a preposition.

> <u>Who</u> discovered this?
> <u>Who</u> did he marry?
> <u>Who</u> did you dance with?

In formal English, 'whom' is used as the object of a verb or preposition. The preposition always comes in front of 'whom'.

Whom did you see?
For whom were they supposed to do it?

You use 'whose' to ask which person something belongs to or is related to. 'Whose' can be the subject or the object.

Whose is nearer?
Whose did you prefer, hers or mine?

2 You use 'which' to ask about one person or thing, out of a number of people or things. 'Which' can be the subject or object.

Which is your son?
Which does she want?

3 You use 'what' to ask about things, for example about actions and events. 'What' can be the subject or object.

What has happened to him?
What is he selling?
What will you talk about?

You use 'what...for' to ask about the reason for an action, or the purpose of an object.

What are you going there *for*?
What are those lights *for*?

4 You use 'how' to ask about the way in which something happens or is done.

How did you know we were coming?
How are you going to get home?

You also use 'how' to ask about the way a person or thing feels or looks.

'*How* are you?' – 'Well, *how* do I look?'

---

5 'How' is also used:

- with adjectives to ask about the degree of quality that someone or something has

  How good are you at Maths?
  How hot shall I make the curry?

- with adjectives such as 'big', 'old', and 'far' to ask about size, age, and distance

  How old are your children?
  How far is it to Montreal from here?

Note that you do not normally use 'how small', 'how young', or 'how near'.

- with adverbs such as 'long' and 'often' to ask about time, or 'well' to ask about abilities

  How long have you lived here?
  How well can you read?

- with 'many' and 'much' to ask about the number or amount of something

> *How many* were there?
> *How much* did he tell you?

---

6 You use 'when' to ask about points in time or periods of time, 'why' to ask about the reason for an action, and 'where' to ask about place and direction.

> *When* are you coming home?
> *When* were you in London?
> *Why* are you here?
> *Where* is the station?
> *Where* are you going?

You can also ask about direction using 'which direction...in' or 'which way'.

> *Which direction* did he go *in*?
> *Which way* did he go?

Unit 7: Question tags: forms

Main points

- You add a question tag to a statement to turn it into a question.
- A question tag consists of a verb and a pronoun. The verb in a question tag is always an auxiliary, a modal, or a form of the main verb 'be'.
- With a positive statement, you usually use a negative question tag containing a short form ending in '-n't'.
- With a negative statement, you always use a positive question tag.

1   A question tag is a short phrase that is added to the end of a statement to turn it into a 'yes/no'-question. You use question tags when you want to ask someone to confirm or disagree with what you are saying, or when you want to sound more polite. Question tags are rarely used in formal written English.

> He's very friendly, _isn't he_?
> You haven't seen it before, _have you_?

2   You form a question tag by using an

auxiliary, a modal, or a form of the main verb 'be', followed by a pronoun. The pronoun refers to the subject of the statement.

> David's school is quite nice, <u>isn't it</u>?
> She made a really remarkable recovery, <u>didn't she</u>?
> I should give her a ring, <u>shouldn't I</u>?

3 If the statement contains an auxiliary or modal, the same auxiliary or modal is used in the question tag.

> Jill<u>'s</u> coming tomorrow, <u>isn't she</u>?
> You <u>did</u>n't know I was an artist, <u>did you</u>?
> You<u>'ve</u> never been to Benidorm, <u>have you</u>?
> You <u>will</u> stay in touch, <u>won't you</u>?

4 If the statement does not contain an auxiliary, a modal, or 'be' as a main verb, you use 'do', 'does', or 'did' in the question tag.

> You <u>like</u> it here, <u>don't you</u>?
> Sally still <u>works</u> there, <u>doesn't she</u>?
> He <u>played</u> for Ireland, <u>did</u>n't he?

5 If the statement contains the present simple or past simple of 'be' as a main verb, the same form of the verb 'be' is used in the question tag.

It _is_ quite warm, _isn't_ it?
They _are_ coming, _aren't_ they?
They _were_ really rude, _weren't_ they?

---

6 If the statement contains the simple present or simple past of 'have' as a main verb, you usually use 'do', 'does', or 'did' in the question tag.

He _has_ a problem, _doesn't_ he?
She _had_ a bath yesterday, _didn't_ she?

You can also use the same form of 'have' in the question tag.

She _has_ a large house, _hasn't_ she?
You _haven't_ any stamps, _have_ you?

---

7 With a positive statement you normally use a negative question tag, formed by adding '-n't' to the verb.

You _like_ Ralph a lot, _don't_ you?
She _thinks_ she's clever, _doesn't_ she?
They _are_ beautiful, _aren't_ they?

Note that the negative question tag with 'I' and the verb 'to be' is 'aren't'.

_I'm_ a fool, _aren't_ I?

8 With a negative statement you always use a positive question tag.

> It _doesn't_ work, _does_ it?
> You _won't_ tell anyone else, _will_ you?
> You _haven't_ been there before, _have_ you?

Unit 8: Question tags: uses

Main points

- You can use negative statements with positive question tags to make requests.
- You use positive statements with positive question tags to show reactions.
- You use some question tags to make imperatives more polite.

1 You can use a negative statement and a positive question tag to ask people for things, or to ask for help or information.

> You _wouldn't_ sell it to me, _would_ you?
> You _won't_ tell anyone else this, _will_ you?

2 When you want to show your reaction to what someone has just said, for example by expressing interest, surprise, doubt, or anger, you use a positive statement with a positive question tag.

> You_'ve_ been to North America before, _have you_?
> You _fell_ on your back, _did you_?

I borrowed your car last night. – Oh, you <u>did</u>, <u>did you</u>?

3   When you use an imperative, you can be more polite by adding one of the following question tags.

| will you | won't you | would you |

<u>See</u> that she gets safely back, <u>won't you</u>?
<u>Look</u> at that, <u>would you</u>?

When you use a negative imperative, you can only use 'will you' as a question tag.

<u>Don't</u> tell Howard, <u>will you</u>?

'Will you' and 'won't you' can also be used to emphasize anger or impatience. 'Can't you' is also used in this way.

Oh, hurry up, <u>will you</u>!
For goodness sake be quiet, <u>can't you</u>!

4   You use the question tag 'shall we' when you make a suggestion using 'let's'.

<u>Let's</u> forget it, <u>shall we</u>?

You use the question tag 'shall I' after 'I'll'.

<u>I'll</u> tell you, <u>shall I</u>?

5 You use 'they' in question tags after 'anybody', 'anyone', 'everybody', 'everyone', 'nobody', 'no one', 'somebody' or 'someone'.

> _Everyone_ will be leaving on Friday, won't _they_?
> _Nobody_ had bothered to plant new ones, had _they_?

You use 'it' in question tags after 'anything', 'everything', 'nothing', or 'something'.

> _Nothing_ matters now, does _it_?
> _Something_ should be done, shouldn't _it_?

You use 'there' in question tags after 'there is', 'there are', 'there was', or 'there were'.

> _There's_ a new course out now, isn't _there_?

6 When you are replying to a question tag, your answer refers to the statement, not the question tag.

If you want to confirm a positive statement, you say 'yes'. For example, if you have finished a piece of work and someone says to you 'You've finished that, haven't you?', the answer is 'yes'.

> 'It _became_ stronger, didn't it?' – '_Yes_, it did.'

If you want to disagree with a positive statement, you say 'no'. For example, if you have not finished your work and someone says 'You've finished that, haven't you?', the answer is 'no'.

>'You've just seen a performance of the play, haven't you?' – 'No, not yet.'

If you want to confirm a negative statement, you say 'no'. For example, if you have not finished your work and someone says 'You haven't finished that, have you?', the answer is 'no'.

>'You didn't know that, did you?' – 'No.'

If you want to disagree with a negative statement, you say 'yes'. For example, if you have finished a piece of work and someone says 'You haven't finished that, have you?', the answer is 'yes'.

>'You haven't been there, have you?' – 'Yes, I have.'

Unit 9: Indirect questions

Main points

- You use indirect questions to ask for information or help.
- In indirect questions, the subject of the question comes before the verb.
- You can use 'if' or 'whether' in indirect questions.

1 When you ask someone for information, you can use an indirect question beginning with a phrase such as 'Could you tell me...' or 'Do you know...'.

   Could you tell me how far it is to the nearest bank?
   Do you know where Jane is?

2 When you want to ask someone politely to do something, you can use an indirect question after 'I wonder'.

   I wonder if you can help me.
   I was wondering whether you could give me some information?

You also use 'I wonder' followed by an indirect question to indicate what you are thinking about.

I wonder what she'll look like.
I wonder which hotel it was.
I just wonder what you make of all that.
I wonder how he'll feel when we tell him.

---

3 In indirect questions, the subject of the
question comes before the verb, just as it
does in affirmative sentences.

Do you know where Jane is?
I wonder if you can help me.
She asked me why I was late.

---

4 You do not normally use the auxiliary 'do'
in indirect questions.

*Can you remember when they open on
Sundays?*
I wonder what he feels about it.

The auxiliary 'do' can be used in indirect
questions, but only for emphasis, or to
make a contrast with something that has
already been said. It is not put before the
subject as in direct questions.

*I was beginning to wonder if he does do
anything.*
*He wondered whether it really did make
any difference to the outcome.*

5 You use 'if' or 'whether' to introduce indirect questions.

> *I wonder <u>if</u> you'd look after the children tonight?*
> *Do you know <u>if</u> there's a lot of crime in the area?*
> *Can you tell me <u>whether</u> you went to Leeds at all in the last year?*
> *I'm writing to ask <u>whether</u> you would care to come and visit us.*

'Whether' is used especially when there is a choice of possibilities.

> *I wonder <u>whether</u> it is the police or just a neighbour.*
> *I wonder <u>whether</u> that is good for him or not.*
> *He didn't know <u>whether</u> I was going to back down or not.*
> *Choosing shrubs to plant against the walls of a house is tricky because you have to think <u>whether</u> the wall is sunny or shady.*

Note that you can put 'or not' immediately
after 'whether', but not immediately after
'if'.

*I wonder <u>whether or not</u> we are so different
from our ancestors.*
*Even optimists wonder <u>if</u> property prices can
keep on rising.*

Unit 10: Short answers

Main points

- A short answer uses an auxiliary, a modal, or the main verb 'be'.
- A short answer can be in the form of a statement or a question.

1   Short answers are very common in spoken English. For example, when someone asks you a 'yes/no'-question, you can give a short answer by using a pronoun with an auxiliary, modal, or the main verb 'be'. You usually put 'yes' or 'no' before the short answer.

> '<u>Does</u> she still want to come?' – 'Yes, <u>she does</u>.'
> '<u>Can</u> you imagine what it might feel like?' – 'No, <u>I can't</u>.'
> '<u>Are</u> you married?' – '<u>I am</u>.'

Note that a short answer such as 'Yes, I will' is more polite or friendly than just 'Yes', or than repeating all the words used in the question. People often repeat all the words used in the question when they feel angry or impatient.

'Will you have finished by lunchtime?' – 'Yes,
I will have finished by lunchtime.'

---

2 You can also use short answers to agree or
disagree with what someone says.

<u>You don't</u> like Joan?' – 'No, <u>I don't.</u>'
'<u>I'm not coming</u> with you.' – 'Yes, <u>you are.</u>'

If the statement that you are commenting
on does not contain an auxiliary, modal,
or the main verb 'be', you use a form of 'do'
in the short answer.

'He never comes on time.' – 'Oh yes <u>he does.</u>'

---

3 You often reply to what has been said by
using a short question.

'He's not in Japan now.' – 'Oh, <u>isn't he?</u>'
'He gets free meals.' – '<u>Does he?</u>'

Note that questions like these are not
always asked to get information, but are
often used to express your reaction to
what has been said, for example to show
interest or surprise.

'Dad doesn't help me at all.' – '<u>Doesn't he?</u>
Why not?'
'Penny has been climbing before.' – 'Oh,
<u>has she?</u> When was that?'

4 If you want to show that you definitely agree with a positive statement that someone has just made, you can use a negative short question.

'Well, that was very nice.' – 'Yes, <u>wasn't it</u>?'

5 When you want to ask for more information, you can use a 'wh'-word on its own or with a noun as a short answer.

'He saw a snake.' – '<u>Where</u>?'
'He knew my cousin.' – '<u>Which cousin</u>?'

You can also use 'Which one' and 'Which ones'.

'Can you pass me the cup?' – '<u>Which one</u>?'

6 Sometimes a statement about one person also applies to another person. When this is the case, you can use a short answer with 'so' for positive statements, and with 'neither' or 'nor' for negative statements, using the same verb that was used in the statement.

You use 'so', 'neither', or 'nor' with an auxiliary, modal, or the main verb 'be'. The verb comes before the subject.

'You were different then.' – '<u>So were you</u>.'
'I don't usually have breakfast.' – '<u>Neither do I</u>.'
'I can't do it.' – '<u>Nor can I</u>.'

You can use 'not either' instead of 'neither', in which case the verb comes after the subject.

'He doesn't understand.' – 'We don't either.'

---

7 You often use 'so' in short answers after verbs such as 'think', 'hope', 'expect', 'imagine', and 'suppose', when you think that the answer to the question is 'yes'.

'You'll be home at six?' – 'I hope so.'
'So it was worth doing?' – 'I suppose so.'

You use 'I'm afraid so' when you are sorry that the answer is 'yes'.

'Is it raining?' – 'I'm afraid so.'

With 'suppose', 'think', 'imagine', or 'expect' in short answers, you also form negatives with 'so'.

'Will I see you again?' – 'I don't suppose so.'
'Is Barry Knight a golfer?' – 'No, I don't think so.'

However, you say 'I hope not' and 'I'm afraid not'.

'It isn't empty, is it?' – 'I hope not.'

Unit 11: Sentences with 'not'

Main points

- 'Not' is often shortened to '-n't' and added to some verbs.
- You put 'not' after the first verb in the verb phrase, or you use a short form.

1 In spoken English and in informal written English, 'not' is often shortened to '-n't' and added to an auxiliary, a modal, or a form of the main verb 'be'.

> I <u>haven't</u> heard from her recently.
> I <u>wasn't</u> angry.

Here is a list of short forms.

isn't	haven't	don't	can't	shan't	daren't
aren't	hasn't	doesn't	couldn't	shouldn't	needn't
wasn't	hadn't	didn't	mightn't	won't	
weren't			mustn't	wouldn't	
			oughtn't		

If the verb is already shortened, you cannot add '-n't'.

> It's <u>not</u> easy.
> I've <u>not</u> had time.

You cannot add '-n't' to 'am'. You use 'I'm not'.

  I'm not excited.

---

2 If the verb phrase has more than one word, you put 'not' after the first word, or you use a short form.

  I was not smiling.
  He hadn't attended many meetings.
  They might not notice.
  I haven't been playing football recently.

---

3 If the sentence only contains a main verb other than 'be', you use the auxiliary 'do'.

You use 'do not', 'does not', 'did not', or a short form, followed by the base form of the main verb.

  They do not need to talk.
  He does not speak English very well.
  I didn't know that.

Note that if the main verb is 'do', you still use a form of 'do' as an auxiliary.

  They didn't do anything about it.

---

4 If the main verb is the present or past simple of 'be', you put 'not' immediately after it, or you use a short form.

It <u>is not</u> difficult to understand.
It<u>'s not</u> the same, is it?
He <u>wasn't</u> a very good actor.

---

5 If the main verb is 'have', you usually use a form of 'do' as an auxiliary.

They <u>don't have</u> any money.

You can also use a short form.

He <u>hadn't</u> enough money.

---

6 You can put 'not' in front of an '-ing' form or a 'to'-infinitive.

We stood there, <u>not knowing</u> what to do.
Try <u>not to worry</u>.

---

7 In negative questions, you use a short form.

Why <u>didn't</u> she win at the Olympics?
<u>Hasn't</u> he put on weight?
<u>Aren't</u> you bored?

---

8 You can use a negative question:

• to express your feelings, for example to show that you are surprised or disappointed

Hasn't he done it yet?

- in exclamations

  Isn't the weather awful!

- when you think you know something and you just want someone to agree with you

  'Aren't you Joanne's brother?' – 'Yes, I am.'

---

9 Note the meaning of 'yes' and 'no' in answers to negative questions.

  '<u>Isn't</u> Tracey going to get a bit bored in Birmingham?'
  – 'Yes.' (She is going to get bored.)
  – 'No.' (She is not going to get bored.)

Unit 12: Negative words

Main points

- A negative sentence contains a negative word.
- You do not normally use two negative words in the same clause.

1 Negative statements contain a negative word.

not	nobody	neither	never	no one
nor	no		nothing	none	nowhere

→ See Unit 11 for negative statements using 'not'.

2 You use 'never' to say that something was not the case at any time, or will not be the case at any time.

If the verb phrase has more than one word, you put 'never' after the first word.

> I*'ve never* had such a horrible meal.
> He *could never* trust her again.

3 If the only verb in the sentence is the present simple or past simple of any main verb except 'be', you put 'never' before the verb.

She <u>never goes</u> abroad.
He <u>never went</u> to university.

If the only verb in the sentence is the present simple or past simple of the main verb 'be', you normally put 'never' after the verb.

He'<u>s never</u> late.
There <u>were never</u> any people in the house.

You can also use 'never' at the beginning of an imperative sentence.

<u>Never</u> walk alone late at night.

---

4 You use 'no' before a noun to say that something does not exist or is not available.

He has given <u>no</u> reason for his decision.
The island has <u>no</u> trees at all.

Note that if there is another negative word in the clause, you use 'any', not 'no'.

It won'<u>t</u> do <u>any</u> good.

---

5 You use 'none' or 'none of' to say that there is not even one thing or person, or not even a small amount of something.

You can't go to a college here because there are <u>none</u> in this area.

'Where's the coffee?' – 'There's <u>none</u> left.'
<u>None of</u> us understood the play.

→ See Unit 32 for more information on
'none' and 'none of'.

6   You also use 'nobody', 'no one', 'nothing',
and 'nowhere' in negative statements.

You use 'nobody' or 'no one' to talk about
people.

<u>Nobody</u> in her house knows any English.
<u>No one</u> knew.

'No one' can also be written 'no-one'.

There's <u>no-one</u> here.

You use 'nothing' to talk about things.

There's <u>nothing</u> you can do.

You use 'nowhere' to talk about places.

There's almost <u>nowhere</u> left to go.

→ See Unit 25 for more information about
these words.

7   You do not normally use two negative
words in the same clause. For example,
you do not say 'Nobody could see nothing'.
You say 'Nobody could see anything'.

You use 'anything', 'anyone', 'anybody', and
'anywhere' instead of 'nothing', 'no one',

'nobody', and 'nowhere' when the clause already contains a negative word.

> <u>No-one</u> can find Howard or Barbara <u>anywhere</u>.
>
> I could <u>never</u> discuss <u>anything</u> with them.

8   The only negative words that are often used together in the same clause are 'neither' and 'nor'. You use 'neither' and 'nor' together to say that two alternatives are not possible, not likely, or not true.

> <u>Neither</u> Margaret <u>nor</u> John was there.
>
> They had <u>neither</u> food <u>nor</u> money.

Unit 13: Broad negatives

Main points

- A broad negative is an adverb that makes a statement almost totally negative. For example, if you say that something is 'hardly surprising', you mean that it is not very surprising.

- Broad negatives usually come before the main verb, but they come after 'be' as a main verb.

1 Broad negatives are adverbs that are used to make a statement almost totally negative. Here is a list of broad negatives:

barely	hardly	rarely	scarcely	seldom

2 If the main verb is the present simple or past simple of any verb except 'be', the broad negative usually comes in front of the main verb.

> He _seldom bathed_.
> John _barely spoke_ to me.

3 If the main verb is the present simple or past simple of 'be', the broad negative usually comes after it.

> *Change <u>is seldom</u> easy.*
> *It <u>was hardly</u> surprising that she left.*

---

4 If there is an auxiliary or modal, you put the broad negative after it.

> *I <u>could barely hear</u> him.*
> *Problems <u>were rarely discussed</u> in our house.*

---

5 If you make a question tag out of a statement that contains a broad negative, the tag on the end of the statement is normally positive.

> *She's <u>hardly</u> the right person for the job,*
> <u>*is she*</u>*?*
> *You <u>rarely</u> see that sort of thing these days,*
> <u>*do you*</u>*?*

→ See Unit 7 for information about question tags.

---

6 If you want to say that there is very little of something, you can use a broad negative with 'any' or with a word that begins with 'any-'.

> *He spoke <u>barely any</u> English.*
> *<u>Hardly anybody</u> came.*

Unit 14: Countable nouns

Main points

- Countable nouns have two forms, singular and plural.
- They can be used with numbers.
- Singular countable nouns always take a determiner.
- Plural countable nouns do not need a determiner.
- Singular countable nouns take a singular verb and plural countable nouns take a plural verb.

1 In English, some things are thought of as individual items that can be counted directly. The nouns which refer to these countable things are called countable nouns. Most nouns in English are countable nouns.
→ See Unit 16 for information on uncountable nouns.

2 Countable nouns have two forms. The singular form refers to one thing or person.

   ...a book ... ...the teacher...

The plural form refers to more than one thing or person.

... _books_ ... ...some _teachers_ ...

---

3 You add '-s' to form the plural of most nouns.

book → books	school → schools

You add '-es' to nouns ending in '-ss', '-ch', '-s', '-sh', or '-x'.

class → classes	watch → watches
gas → gases	dish → dishes
fox → foxes	

Some nouns ending in '-o' add '-s', and some add '-es'.

photo → photos	piano → pianos
hero → heroes	potato → potatoes

Nouns ending in a consonant and '-y' change to '-ies'.

country → countries	lady → ladies
party → parties	victory → victories

Nouns ending in a vowel and '-y' add an '-s'.

boy → boys	day → days
key → keys	valley → valleys

Some common nouns have irregular plurals.

child → children	foot → feet
man → men	mouse → mice
tooth → teeth	woman → women

⚠ BE CAREFUL

Some nouns that end in '-s' are uncountable nouns, for example 'athletics' and 'physics'.
→ See Unit 16.

---

4 Countable nouns can be used with numbers.

> ... one table... ... two cats...
> ... three hundred pounds.

5 Singular countable nouns cannot be used alone, but always take a determiner such as 'a', 'another', 'every', or 'the'.

> We've killed _a_ pig.
> He was eating _another_ apple.
> I parked _the_ car over there.

---

6 Plural countable nouns can be used with or without a determiner. They do not take a determiner when they refer to things or people in general.

Does the hotel have <u>large rooms</u>?
The film is not suitable for <u>children</u>.

Plural countable nouns do take a determiner when they refer precisely to particular things or people.

<u>Our computers</u> are very expensive.
<u>These cakes</u> are delicious.

→ See Unit 28 for more information on determiners.

7 When a countable noun is the subject of a verb, a singular countable noun takes a singular verb.

My <u>son likes</u> playing football.
The <u>address</u> on the letter <u>was</u> wrong.

A plural countable noun takes a plural verb.

Bigger <u>cars cost</u> more.
I thought more <u>people were</u> coming.

→ See also Unit 15 on collective nouns.

Unit 15: Singular and plural

Main points

- Singular nouns are used only in the singular, always with a determiner.
- Plural nouns are used only in the plural, some with a determiner.
- Collective nouns can be used with singular or plural verbs.

1 Some nouns are used in particular meanings in the singular with a determiner, like countable nouns, but are not used in the plural with that meaning. They are often called 'singular nouns'.

Some of these nouns are normally used with 'the' because they refer to things that are unique.

air	country	countryside	dark
daytime	end	future	ground
moon	past	sea	seaside
sky	sun	wind	world

The sun was shining.
I am scared of _the dark_.

Other singular nouns are normally used with 'a' because they refer to actions or activities that we usually talk about one at a time.

bath	chance	drink	fight
go	jog	move	rest
ride	run	shower	snooze
start	walk	wash	

I went upstairs and had <u>a wash</u>.
Why don't we go for <u>a walk</u>?

2 Some nouns are used in particular meanings in the plural with or without determiners, like countable nouns, but are not used in the singular with that meaning. They are often called 'plural nouns'.

His <u>clothes</u> looked terribly dirty.
<u>Troops</u> are being sent in today.

Some of these nouns are always used with determiners.

| activities | authorities | feelings | likes |
| pictures | sights | travels | |

I went to <u>the pictures</u> with Tina.
You hurt <u>his feelings</u>.

Some are usually used without determiners.

| airs expenses goods refreshments riches |

Refreshments are available inside.
They have agreed to pay for travel and
expenses.

⚠ BE CAREFUL

'Police' is a plural noun, but does not end
in '-s'.

The police were informed immediately.

---

3 A small group of plural nouns refer to
single items that have two linked parts.
They refer to tools that people use or
things that people wear.

binoculars	pincers	pliers	scales
scissors	shears	tweezers	glasses
jeans	knickers	pants	pyjamas
shorts	tights	trousers	

She was wearing brown trousers.
These scissors are sharp.

You can use 'a pair of' to make it clear you
are talking about one item, or a number
with 'pairs of' when you are talking about
several items.

I was sent out to buy a pair of scissors.
Liza had given me three pairs of jeans.

Note that you also use 'a pair of' with
words such as 'gloves', 'shoes', and 'socks'
that you often talk about in twos.

4 With some nouns that refer to a group of people or things, the same form can be used with singular or plural verbs, because you can think of the group as a unit or as individuals. Similarly, you can use singular or plural pronouns to refer back to them. These nouns are often called 'collective nouns'.

army	audience	committee	company
crew	enemy	family	flock
gang	government	group	herd
media	navy	press	public
staff	team		

Our little <u>group is</u> complete again.
Our <u>family isn't</u> poor any more.
The other <u>group were</u> late.
My <u>family are</u> perfectly normal.

The names of many organizations and sports teams are also collective nouns, but are normally used with plural verbs in spoken English.

<u>The BBC is</u> showing the programme on Saturday.
<u>The BBC are</u> planning to use the new satellite.
<u>Liverpool is</u> leading 1–0.
<u>Liverpool are</u> attacking again.

Unit 16: Uncountable nouns

Main points

- Uncountable nouns have only one form, and take a singular verb.
- They are not used with 'a', or with numbers.
- Some nouns can be both uncountable nouns and countable nouns.

1 English speakers think that some things cannot be counted directly. The nouns which refer to these uncountable things are called uncountable nouns. Uncountable nouns often refer to:

substances:	coal food ice iron rice steel water
human qualities:	courage cruelty honesty patience
feelings:	anger happiness joy pride relief respect
activities:	aid help sleep travel work
abstract ideas:	beauty death freedom fun life luck

The donkey needed <u>food</u> and <u>water</u>.
I lost <u>patience</u> and left.
I was greeted with shouts of <u>joy</u>.
All prices include <u>travel</u> to and from London.
We talked for hours about <u>freedom</u>.

➜ See Unit 14 for information on
countable nouns.

---

2 Uncountable nouns have only one form.
They do not have a plural form.

I needed <u>help</u> with my homework.
*The children had great <u>fun</u> playing with
the puppets.*

⚠ **BE CAREFUL**

Some nouns which are uncountable
nouns in English have plurals in other
languages.

advice	baggage	equipment
furniture	homework	information
knowledge	luggage	machinery
money	news	traffic

We want to spend more <u>money</u> on roads.
*Soldiers carried so much <u>equipment</u> that
they were barely able to move.*

3 Some uncountable nouns end in '-s' and
therefore look like plural countable nouns.

They usually refer to:

subjects of study:	maths physics
activities:	athletics gymnastics
games:	cards darts
illnesses:	measles mumps

Maths is too difficult for me.
Measles is in most cases a harmless illness.

4   When an uncountable noun is the subject of a verb, it takes a singular verb.

Electricity *is* dangerous.
Food *was* very expensive in those days.

5   Uncountable nouns are not used with 'a'.

They resent having to pay *money* to people like me.
My father started *work* when he was ten.

Uncountable nouns are used with 'the' when they refer to something that is specified or known.

I am interested in *the education of young children*.
She spent *the money that Hilary had given her*.

6   Uncountable nouns are not used with numbers. However, you can often refer to

a quantity of something which is expressed by an uncountable noun, by using a word like 'some'.
→ See Unit 28.

> *Could you buy <u>some bread</u> when you go to town?*
> *Let me give you <u>some advice</u>.*

Some uncountable nouns that refer to food or drink can be countable nouns when they refer to quantities of the food or drink.

> *Do you like <u>coffee</u>?* (uncountable)
> *We asked for <u>two coffees</u>.* (countable)

Uncountable nouns are often used with expressions such as 'a loaf of', 'packets of', or 'a piece of', to talk about a quantity or an item. 'A bit of' is common in spoken English.

> *I bought <u>two loaves of bread</u> yesterday.*
> *He gave me <u>a</u> very good <u>piece of advice</u>.*
> *They own <u>a bit of land</u> near Cambridge.*

7 Some nouns are uncountable nouns when they refer to something in general and countable nouns when they refer to a particular instance of something.

> *<u>Victory</u> was now assured.* (uncountable)
> *In 1960, the party won <u>a convincing victory</u>.* (countable)

Unit 17: Proper nouns and common nouns

Main points

- Common nouns are nouns that refer to a class of people, objects, substances, or concepts.
- Proper nouns are nouns that refer to particular named people, places, or things.
- Proper nouns are always spelled with a capital letter.

1 Common nouns are nouns that refer to a class of people, objects, substances, or concepts. They are not spelled with a capital letter unless they begin a sentence.

> A young <u>woman</u> was waiting outside the <u>station</u>.
> I never told my <u>parents</u> anything about <u>school</u>.
> My <u>car</u> was parked just across from the <u>building</u>.

2 Proper nouns are nouns that refer to particular named people, places, or things. They are always spelled with a capital letter.

We spent a day in <u>New York</u> and saw the <u>Statue of Liberty</u>.
I saw <u>Jenny</u> on <u>Saturday</u>.
He was born in <u>Poland</u> but later moved to <u>France</u>.

3 People's names are proper nouns.

Michael Hall
Maria Piotrowski
Jason
Mrs Smith
Mr Hernandez

4 Titles (polite labels that show someone's status or job) are proper nouns.

President Obama
Dr Sanchez
Sir John Soane
Professor Kay
Councillor Smith
Lady Bracknell
Rabbi Greenburn

---

5 Countries, cities, streets, rivers, mountains, and other geographical items are proper nouns.

> *Italy*
> *San Francisco*
> *Baker Street*
> *Seventh Avenue*
> *The Danube*
> *Mount Everest*
> *Lake Superior*
> *The Maldives*
> *North Africa*
> *East Anglia*

---

6 Days of the week, months of the year, and annual festivals are proper nouns.

> *Monday*
> *April*
> *Christmas*
> *New Year's Day*
> *Bonfire Night*
> *Diwali*

---

7 The names of organizations, institutions, ships, newspapers, magazines, books, plays, paintings, and other unique things are also proper nouns.

The British Broadcasting Corporation
Harvard University
Marks and Spencer
The Wall Street Journal
A Midsummer Night's Dream
The Mona Lisa

Unit 18: Compound nouns

Main points

- A compound noun is a noun that is formed from two or more words.
- Compound nouns can be written as separate words, as single words, or with a hyphen.
- The plural form of a compound noun is usually the plural form of the last word.
- The meaning of a compound noun is sometimes different from the words it consists of.

1 A compound noun is a noun that is formed from two or more words.

> I have a bad _headache_.
> My _mother-in-law_ came to stay.

2 Some compound nouns are written as separate words, for example 'address book' and 'driving licence'.

Some compound nouns are written with hyphens, for example 'mother-in-law' and 't-shirt'.

Some compound nouns, especially frequent ones, are written as one word, for example 'wallpaper' and 'snowflake'.

In some cases, there are different options. For example, you can write either 'air conditioning' or 'air-conditioning'. Check in a dictionary to find out how the compound noun is normally written.

3 In most compound nouns, the last word is a noun. In many cases, the first word is another noun or an adjective. The first word can also be a verb or a particle.

> I'll meet you at the <u>bus stop</u>. (noun + noun)
> We installed some new <u>software</u>. (adjective + noun)
> Have you had <u>breakfast</u> yet? (verb + noun)
> A crowd of <u>onlookers</u> gathered outside the church. (particle + noun)

Some compound nouns are related to phrasal verbs. These are sometimes written with a hyphen, and sometimes as one word. They are rarely written as separate words.

> I think there's been a <u>mix-up</u>.
> The singer is making a <u>comeback</u>.

→ See Unit 63 for information about phrasal verbs.

4 The plural form of a compound noun is usually the plural form of the last word.

> *Several <u>health centres</u>, <u>post offices</u>, and <u>police stations</u> have been shut down.*
> *They sell <u>dishwashers</u> and <u>washing machines</u>.*

Compound nouns that are related to phrasal verbs usually have a plural form ending in '-s'.

> *There are some <u>drawbacks</u> to the proposal.*
> *Several car <u>break-ins</u> were reported.*

There are a few exceptions. The most common are 'runner-up', which has the plural form 'runners-up', and 'passer-by', which has the plural form 'passers-by'.

If the compound noun consists of two nouns linked by 'of' or 'in', the first noun becomes plural.

> *We saw several <u>birds of prey</u>, including two hawks and an eagle.*
> *She was treated badly by her <u>sisters-in-law</u>.*

Some compound nouns are uncountable or singular, and do not have plural forms.

> *We like to eat in the <u>open air</u>.*
> *Do you sell <u>writing paper</u>?*

5 In some cases, the meaning of a compound noun is not obvious from the words it consists of.

For example, someone's 'mother tongue' is not the tongue of their mother but the language they learn as a child. An 'old hand' is not a hand that is old but a person who is experienced at doing a particular job.

Unit 19: Adjectives used as nouns

Main points

- You can use adjectives as nouns when you want to talk about groups of people with the same quality, for example 'the poor' and 'the elderly'.
- You never add '-s' to these adjectives.

1 When you talk about groups of people who share the same characteristic or quality, you can use 'the' followed by an adjective. For example, instead of saying 'poor people', you can say 'the poor'.

> *Working with _the young_ is very rewarding.*
> *They provide care for _the sick_, _the aged_,*
> *_the unemployed_ and _the poor_.*

Note that you never add '-s' to the adjective, even though it always refers to more than one person.

2 When the adjective being used as a noun is the subject of a verb, you use a plural form of the verb.

> *_The rich have_ benefited much more than the poor.*

The elderly are usually very careful with
their money.

3 If you want to talk about a more specific
group of people, you put an adverb or
another adjective in front of the adjective
that is being used as a noun.

*This problem affects the very old and
the very young.*
*The urban poor and the rural poor face
different problems.*

4 If you mention two groups, you
sometimes omit 'the'.

*The study compared the diets of rich and
poor in several countries.*
*We want to break down the barriers between
young and old.*

5 Nationality adjectives that end in '-ch',
'-sh', '-se', or '-ss' can be used as nouns, unless
there is a separate noun for the people.
For example, French people are referred
to as 'the French' but Polish people are
usually referred to as 'Poles' or 'the Poles'.

*For many years, the Japanese have been very
successful in developing technology.*
*Britons are the biggest consumers of
chocolate after the Swiss and the Irish.*

Unit 20: Personal pronouns

Main points

- You use personal pronouns to refer back to something or someone that has already been mentioned.

- You also use personal pronouns to refer to people and things directly.

- There are two sets of personal pronouns: subject pronouns and object pronouns.

- You can use 'you' and 'they' to refer to people in general.

1 When something or someone has already been mentioned, you refer to them again by using a pronoun.

> John took _the book_ and opened _it_.
> He rang _Mary_ and invited _her_ to dinner.
> 'Have you been to _London_?' – 'Yes, _it_ was very crowded.'
> _My father_ is tall – _he_ is over six feet.

In English, 'he' and 'she' normally refer to people, occasionally to animals, but very rarely to things.

2 You use a pronoun to refer directly to people or things that are present or are involved in the situation you are in.

> Where shall <u>we</u> meet, Sally?
> <u>I</u> do the washing; <u>he</u> does the cooking; <u>we</u> share the washing-up.
> Send <u>us</u> a card so <u>we</u>'ll know where <u>you</u> are.

3 There are two sets of personal pronouns, subject pronouns and object pronouns. You use subject pronouns as the subject of a verb.

| I | you | he | she | it | we | they |

Note that 'you' is used for the singular and plural form.

> <u>We</u> are going there later.
> <u>I</u> don't know what to do.

4 You use object pronouns as the direct or indirect object of a verb.

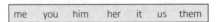

| me | you | him | her | it | us | them |

Note that 'you' is used for the singular and plural form.

> The nurse washed <u>me</u> with cold water.
> The ball hit <u>her</u> in the face.

John showed <u>him</u> the book.
Can you give <u>me</u> some more cake?

Note that, in modern English, you use object pronouns rather than subject pronouns after the verb 'be'.

'Who is it?' – 'It's me.'
There <u>was</u> only John, Baz, and <u>me</u> in the room.

You also use object pronouns as the object of a preposition.

We were all sitting in a cafe <u>with him</u>.
Did you give it <u>to them</u>?

---

5 You can use 'you' and 'they' to talk about people in general.

Drinking too much coffee can give <u>you</u> headache.
<u>They</u> say she's very clever.

---

6 You can use 'it' as an impersonal subject in general statements which refer to the time, the date, or the weather.
→ See Unit 21.

'What time is <u>it</u>?' '<u>It</u>'s half past three.'
<u>It</u> is January 19th.
<u>It</u> is rainy and cold.

You can also use 'it' as the subject or object in general statements about a situation.

> _It_ is too far to walk.
> I like _it_ here. Can we stay a bit longer?

---

7 A singular pronoun usually refers back to a singular noun phrase, and a plural pronoun to a plural noun phrase. However, you can use plural pronouns to refer back to:

- indefinite pronouns, even though they are always followed by a singular verb

  If _anybody comes_, tell _them_ I'm not in.

- collective nouns, even when you have used a singular verb

  His _family was_ waiting in the next room, but _they_ had not yet been informed.

Unit 21: Impersonal subject 'it'

Main points

- You use impersonal 'it' as the subject of a sentence to introduce new information.
- You use 'it' to talk about the time or the date.
- You use 'it' to talk about the weather.
- You use 'it' to express opinions about places, situations, and events.
- 'It' is often used with the passive of reporting verbs to express general beliefs and opinions.

1 'It' is a pronoun. As a personal pronoun it refers back to something that has already been mentioned.

> They learn to speak <u>English</u> before they learn to read <u>it</u>.
> <u>Maybe he changed his mind</u>, but I doubt <u>it</u>.

You can also use 'it' as the subject of a sentence when it does not refer back to anything that has already been mentioned. This impersonal use of 'it' introduces new information, and is used particularly to talk about times, dates, the weather, and personal opinions.

---

2 You use impersonal 'it' with a form of 'be' to talk about the time or the date.

> _It is_ nearly one o'clock.
> _It's_ the sixth of April today.

---

3 You use impersonal 'it' with verbs which refer to the weather:

| drizzle hail pour rain sleet snow thunder |

> _It's_ still _raining_.
> _It snowed_ steadily through the night.
> _It was pouring_ with rain.

You can describe the weather by using 'it' followed by 'be' and an adjective with or without a noun.

> _It's a lovely day._
> _It was very bright._

You can describe a change in the weather by using 'it' followed by 'get' and an adjective.

> _It was getting cold._
> _It's getting dark._

4 You use impersonal 'it', followed by a form of 'be' and an adjective or noun phrase, to express your opinion about a place, a situation, or an event. The adjective or noun phrase can be followed by an adverbial or by an '-ing' clause, a 'to'-infinitive clause, or a 'that'-clause.

> <u>It was</u> terribly <u>cold in the trucks</u>.
> <u>It's fun working</u> for him.
> <u>It was a pleasure to be</u> there.
> <u>It's strange that</u> it hasn't been noticed before.

5 You use 'it' followed by a verb such as 'interest', 'please', 'surprise', or 'upset' which indicates someone's reaction to a fact, situation, or event. The verb is followed by a noun phrase, and a 'that'-clause or a 'to'-infinitive clause.

> <u>It pleases me that</u> he wants to talk about his work.
> <u>It surprised him to realize</u> that he hadn't thought about them until now.

6 You can also use 'it' with the passive of a reporting verb and a 'that'-clause when you want to suggest that an opinion or belief is shared by many people. This use is particularly common in news reports, for example in newspapers, on the radio, or on television.

It was said that he could speak their
language.
Nowadays *it is believed that* the size is
unimportant.
It is thought that about a million puppies
are born each year.

Note that the passive of reporting verbs
can also be used without impersonal 'it'
to express general opinions.

The factories were said to be much worse.
They are believed to be dangerous.

→ See Units 84 and 85 for more
information on reporting verbs.

Unit 22: Impersonal subject 'there'

Main points

- You use 'there' followed by a form of 'be' and a noun phrase to introduce new information.
- You use 'there' with a singular or plural verb, depending on whether the following noun is singular or plural.
- You can also use 'there' with modals.

1 'There' is often an adverb of place.

> Are you comfortable _there_?
> The book is _there_ on the table.

You can also use 'there' as the impersonal subject of a sentence when it does not refer to a place. In this case you use 'there' to introduce new information and to focus on it. After 'there' you use a form of 'be' and a noun phrase.

> _There is work_ to be done.
> _There will be a party_ tonight.
> _There was no damage_.
> _There have been two telephone calls_.

Note that the impersonal subject 'there' is often pronounced without stress, whereas the adverb is almost always stressed.

---

2 You use 'there' as the impersonal subject to talk about:

- the existence or presence of someone or something

  There are two people who might know what happened.
  There are many possibilities.
  There is plenty of bread.

- something that happens

  There was a general election that year.
  There's a meeting every week.
  There was a fierce battle.

- a number or amount

  There are forty of us, I think.
  There is a great deal of anger about his decision.
  There were a lot of people camped there.

---

3 When the noun phrase after the verb is plural, you use a plural verb.

  <u>*There are many reasons*</u> *for this.*
  <u>*There were two men*</u> *in the room.*

You also use a plural verb before phrases such as 'a number (of)', 'a lot (of)', and 'a few (of)'.

> _There were a lot of_ people camped there.
> _There are_ only _a few_ left.

---

4 When the noun phrase after the verb is singular or uncountable, you use a singular verb.

> _There is one point_ we must add here.
> _There isn't enough room_ in here.

You also use a singular verb when you are mentioning more than one person or thing and the first noun after the verb is singular or uncountable.

> _There was a man_ and a woman waiting outside.
> _There was a sofa_ and two chairs.

---

5 You can also use 'there' with a modal, followed by 'be' or 'have been'.

> _There could be_ a problem.
> _There should be_ a change in government.
> _There can't have been_ anybody outside.
> _There must have been_ some mistake.

---

6 In spoken and informal written English, short forms of 'be' or a modal are normally used after 'there'.

There's no danger.
There'll always *be* a future for music.
I knew *there'd be* trouble.
There's been quite a lot of research into it.
I didn't even know *there'd been* an accident.

---

7 You can also use 'there' with 'appear' or 'seem', followed by 'to be' or 'to have been'.

There appears to be a vast amount of confusion on this point.
There don't seem to be many people on campus.
There seems to have been some carelessness.

Unit 23: Demonstrative pronouns

Main point

You use the demonstrative pronouns 'this', 'that', 'these', and 'those' when you are pointing to physical objects or identifying people.

1 You use the demonstrative pronouns 'this', 'that', 'these', and 'those' when you are pointing to physical objects. 'This' and 'these' refer to things near you; 'that' and 'those' refer to things farther away.

> *This is a list of rules.*
> *'I brought you these'. Adam held out a bag of grapes.*
> *That looks interesting.*
> *Those are mine.*

You can also use 'this', 'that', 'these', and 'those' as determiners in front of nouns.
→ See Unit 28.

> *This book was a present from my mother.*
> *When did you buy that hat?*

2 You use 'this', 'that', 'these', and 'those' when you are identifying or introducing people, or asking who they are.

> *Who's <u>this</u>?*
> <u>*These*</u> *are my children, Susan and Paul.*
> *Was <u>that</u> Patrick on the phone?*

3 You use 'this', 'that', 'these', and 'those' to refer back to things that have already been mentioned.

> <u>*That*</u> *was an interesting word you used just now.*
> *More money is being spent on education, and we assume <u>this</u> will continue.*
> *'Let's go to the cinema.' –* '<u>*That's*</u> *a good idea.'*
> <u>*These*</u> *are not easy questions to answer.*

You also use 'this' and 'these' to refer forward to things you are going to mention.

> <u>*This*</u> *is what I want to say: it wasn't my idea.*
> <u>*These*</u> *are the topics we will be looking at next week: how the accident happened, whether it could have been avoided, and who was to blame.*
> <u>*This*</u> *is the important point: you must never see her again.*

Unit 24: Reflexive pronouns

Main points

- Reflexive pronouns can be direct or indirect objects.
- Most transitive verbs can take a reflexive pronoun as object.
- Reflexive pronouns can be the object of a preposition.
- Reflexive pronouns can emphasize a noun or pronoun.

1 The reflexive pronouns are:

singular:	myself yourself himself herself itself
plural:	ourselves yourselves themselves

Note that, unlike 'you' and 'your', there are two forms for the second person: 'yourself' in the singular and 'yourselves' in the plural.

2 You use reflexive pronouns as the direct or indirect object of the verb when you want to say that the object is the same person or thing as the subject of the verb in the same clause.

For example, 'John taught himself' means that John did the teaching and was also the person who was taught, and 'Ann poured herself a drink' means that Ann did the pouring and was also the person that the drink was poured for.

> _She_ stretched _herself_ out on the sofa.
> _The men_ formed _themselves_ into a line.
> _He_ should give _himself_ more time.

Note that although the subject 'you' is omitted in imperatives, you can still use 'yourself' or 'yourselves'.

> Here's the money, go and buy _yourself_ an ice cream.

3 Most transitive verbs can take a reflexive pronoun.

> I _blame myself_ for not paying attention.
> He _introduced himself_ to me.

⚠ BE CAREFUL

Verbs which describe actions that people normally do to themselves do not take reflexive pronouns in English, although they do in some other languages.

> I usually _shave_ before breakfast.
> She _washed_ very quickly and rushed downstairs.

→ See Unit 60 for more information.

4 You use a reflexive pronoun as the object of a preposition when the object of the preposition refers to the same person or thing as the subject of the verb in the same clause.

> *I was thoroughly ashamed <u>of myself</u>.*
> *They are making fools <u>of themselves</u>.*
> *Tell me <u>about yourself</u>.*

Note that you use personal pronouns, not reflexive pronouns, when referring to places. You also use personal pronouns after 'with' meaning 'accompanied by'.

> *<u>You</u> should have your notes <u>in front of you</u>.*
> *<u>He</u> would have to bring Judy <u>with him</u>.*

5 You use reflexive pronouns after nouns or pronouns to emphasize the person or thing that you are referring to.

> *<u>The town itself</u> was so small that it didn't have a bank.*
> *<u>I myself</u> have never read the book.*

6 You use a reflexive pronoun at the end of a clause to emphasize that someone did something without any help from anyone else.

> *She had printed the card <u>herself</u>.*
> *I'll take it down to the police station <u>myself</u>.*
> *Did you make these <u>yourself</u>?*

7 You use reflexive pronouns with 'by' to say:

- that someone does something without any help from other people

  ...when babies start eating their meals
  by themselves.
  She was certain she could manage by herself.

- that someone is alone

  He went off to sit by himself.
  I was there for about six months by myself.

You can also use 'on my own', 'on your own', and so on, to say that someone is alone or does something without any help.

  We were in the park on our own.
  They managed to reach the village on their own.

You can use 'all' for emphasis.

  Did you put those shelves up all by yourself?
  We can't solve this problem all on our own.

⚠ BE CAREFUL

'One another' and 'each other' are not reflexive pronouns.

→ See Unit 61 for more information on 'one another' and 'each other'.

Unit 25: Indefinite pronouns

Main points

- Indefinite pronouns refer to people or things without saying exactly who or what they are.
- When an indefinite pronoun is the subject, it always takes a singular verb.
- You often use a plural pronoun to refer back to an indefinite pronoun.

1 The indefinite pronouns are:

anybody	everybody	nobody	somebody
anyone	everyone	no one	someone
anything	everything	nothing	something

Note that 'no one' is written as two words, or sometimes with a hyphen: 'no-one'.

2 You use indefinite pronouns when you want to refer to people or things without saying exactly who or what they are. The pronouns ending in '-body' and '-one' refer to people, and those ending in '-thing' refer to things.

*I was there for over an hour before
<u>anybody</u> came.
It had to be <u>someone</u> with a car.
Jane said <u>nothing</u> for a moment.*

3 When an indefinite pronoun is the subject,
it always takes a singular verb, even when
it refers to more than one person or thing.

*<u>Everyone knows</u> that.
<u>Everything was</u> fine.
<u>Is anybody</u> there?*

When you refer back to indefinite
pronouns, you use plural pronouns or
possessives, and a plural verb.

*Ask <u>anyone</u>. <u>They'll</u> tell you.
You can't tell <u>somebody</u> why <u>they've</u> failed.
Has <u>everyone</u> finished <u>their</u> lunch?*

⚠ **BE CAREFUL**

Some speakers prefer to use singular
pronouns. They prefer to say 'You can't tell
somebody why he or she has failed'.

4 You can add apostrophe s ('s) to indefinite
pronouns that refer to people.

*She was given a room in <u>someone's</u> studio.
That was <u>nobody's</u> business but mine.*

⚠ **BE CAREFUL**

You do not usually add apostrophe s ('s) to indefinite pronouns that refer to things. You do not say 'something's value'; you say 'the value of something'.

---

5 You use indefinite pronouns beginning with 'some-' in:

- affirmative clauses

  <u>Somebody</u> shouted.
  I want to introduce you to <u>someone</u>.

- questions expecting the answer 'yes'

  Would you like <u>something</u> to drink?
  Can you get <u>someone</u> to do it?

---

6 You use indefinite pronouns beginning with 'any-':

- as the subject or object in statements

  <u>Anyone</u> knows that you need a licence.
  You still haven't told me <u>anything</u>.

- You do not use them as the subject of a negative statement. You do not say 'Anybody can't come in'.

- in both affirmative and negative questions

  Does <u>anybody</u> agree with me?
  Won't <u>anyone</u> help me?

7 If you use an indefinite pronoun beginning with 'no-', you do not use another negative word in the same clause. You do not say 'There wasn't nothing'.

> There was <u>nothing</u> you could do.
> <u>Nobody</u> left, <u>nobody</u> went away.

8 You use the indefinite adverbs 'anywhere', 'everywhere', 'nowhere', and 'somewhere' to talk about places in a general way. 'Nowhere' makes a clause negative.

> I thought I'd seen you <u>somewhere</u>.
> No-one can find Howard or Barbara <u>anywhere</u>.
> There was <u>nowhere</u> to hide.

9 You can use 'else' after indefinite pronouns and adverbs to refer to people, things, or places other than those that have been mentioned.

> <u>Everyone else</u> is downstairs.
> I don't like it here. Let's go <u>somewhere else</u>.

Unit 26: The pronoun 'one'

Main points

- 'One' can be used as a pronoun to refer to one of a group of people or things.
- You use 'one' or 'ones' instead of a noun that has been mentioned or is known.
- In formal English, 'one' is sometimes used as a personal pronoun.

1 Like other numbers, 'one' can be used as a pronoun. It refers to one of a group of people or things.

> *I brought three pens with me but I've lost <u>one</u>.*

2 'One' also has a special use as a pronoun. You use 'one' or 'ones' instead of a noun that has already been mentioned or is known in the situation, usually when you are adding information or contrasting two things of the same kind.

> *<u>My car</u> is <u>the blue one</u>.*
> *Don't you have <u>one</u> with buttons instead of a zip?*
> *Are <u>the new curtains</u> longer than <u>the old ones</u>?*

You can use 'which one' or 'which ones' in questions.

Which one do you prefer?
Which ones were damaged?

You can say 'this one', 'that one', 'these ones', and 'those ones'.

I like _this one_ better.
We'll have _those ones_, thank you.

You can use 'each one' or 'one each', but note that there is a difference in meaning. In the following examples, 'each one' means 'each brother' but 'one each' means 'one for each child'.

I've got three brothers and _each one_ lives in a different country.
I bought the children _one each_.

3 In formal English, people sometimes use 'one' as a personal pronoun to refer to people in general.

One has to think of the practical side of things.
One never knows what to say in such situations.

Unit 27: Possession

Main points

- Possessives and possessive pronouns are used to say that one person or thing belongs to another or is connected with another.

- You use apostrophe s ('s) to say who something belongs to.

- You use phrases with 'of' to say that one person or thing belongs to another or is connected with another.

1 You use possessives to say that a person or thing belongs to another person or thing or is connected with them. The possessives are sometimes called 'possessive adjectives'.

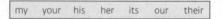

| my | your | his | her | its | our | their |

Note that 'your' is both singular and plural.

I'd been waiting a long time to park <u>my car</u>.
They took off <u>their shoes</u>.

⚠ BE CAREFUL

The possessive 'its' is not spelled with an apostrophe. The form 'it's' with an apostrophe is the short form for 'it is' or 'it has'.

---

2 You put numbers and adjectives after the possessive and in front of the noun.

Their two small children were playing outside.
She got a bicycle on _her sixth birthday_.

---

3 You use a possessive pronoun when you want to refer to a person or thing and to say who that person or thing belongs to or is connected with. The possessive pronouns are:

| mine | yours | his | hers | ours | theirs |

Note that 'yours' is both singular and plural.

_Is that coffee _yours_ or _mine_?
It was his fault, not _theirs_.

⚠ **BE CAREFUL**

There is no possessive pronoun 'its'.

---

4 You can also say who or what something belongs to or is connected with by using a noun with apostrophe s ('s). For example, if John owns a motorbike, you can refer to it as 'John's motorbike'.

_Sylvia put her hand on _John's_ arm.
I like the _car's_ design._

You add apostrophe s ('s) to singular nouns and irregular plural nouns, usually referring to people rather than things.

> I wore my <u>sister's</u> boots.
> <u>Children's</u> birthday parties can be boring.

With plural nouns ending in '-s' you only add the apostrophe (').

> It is not his <u>parents'</u> problem.

You add apostrophe s ('s) to people's names, even when they end in '-s'.

> Could you give me <u>Charles's</u> address?

Note that when you use two or more names linked by 'and', you put the apostrophe s ('s) after the last name.

> They have bought <u>Sue and Tim's</u> car.

---

5 When you want to refer to someone's home, or to some common shops and places of work, you can use apostrophe s ('s) after a name or noun on its own.

> He's round at <u>David's</u>.
> He bought it at the <u>chemist's</u>.
> She must go to the <u>doctor's</u>.

---

6 You can also use apostrophe s ('s) with some expressions of time to identify something, or to say how much time is involved.

Did you see the cartoon in <u>yesterday's</u>
newspaper?
They have four <u>weeks'</u> holiday per year.

---

7 You can use a prepositional phrase
beginning with 'of' to say that one person
or thing belongs to or is connected with
another.

She is the mother <u>of the boy</u> who lives next
door.
Ellen aimlessly turned the pages <u>of her</u>
<u>*magazine*</u>.

After 'of' you can use a possessive
pronoun, or a noun or name with
apostrophe s ('s).

He was an old friend <u>of mine</u>.
That word was a favourite <u>of your father's</u>.
She's a friend <u>of Stephen's</u>.

---

8 You can add 'own' after a possessive, or
a noun or name with apostrophe s ('s),
for emphasis.

<u>*My own*</u> *view is that there are no serious*
problems.
The <u>professor's own</u> answer may be
unacceptable.

Unit 28: Determiners

Main points

- Determiners are used at the beginning of noun phrases.
- You use specific determiners when people know exactly which things or people you are talking about.
- You use general determiners to talk about people or things without saying exactly who or what they are.

1 When you use a determiner, you put it at the beginning of a noun phrase, in front of numbers or adjectives.

> I met _the two Swedish girls_ in London.
> _Our main bedroom_ is through there.
> Have you got _another red card_?

2 When the people or things that you are talking about have already been mentioned, or the people you are talking to know exactly which ones you mean, you use a specific determiner.

> _The_ man began to run towards _the_ boy.
> Young people don't like _these_ operas.
> _Her_ face was very red.

The specific determiners are:

the definite article:	the
demonstratives:	this that these those
possessives:	my your his her its
	our their

Note that 'your' is used both for the singular and plural possessive.

→ See Unit 23 for 'this', 'that', 'these', and 'those' as pronouns.

---

3 When you are mentioning people or things for the first time, or talking about them generally without saying exactly which ones you mean, you use a general determiner.

There was <u>a</u> man in the lift.
We went to <u>an</u> art exhibition.
You can stop at <u>any</u> time you like.
There were <u>several</u> reasons for this.

The general determiners are:

a	all	an	another
any	both	each	either
enough	every	few	fewer
less	little	many	more
most	much	neither	no
other	several	some	

4 Each general determiner is used with particular types of noun, such as:

- singular countable nouns

a	an	another	any	each
either	every	neither	no	

  I got *a postcard* from Susan.
  He opened *another shop*.
  Any big tin container will do.

- plural countable nouns

all	any	both	enough
few	fewer	many	more
most	no	other	several
some			

  There were *few doctors* available.
  Several projects were postponed.
  He spoke *many different languages*.

- uncountable nouns

all	any	enough	less
little	more	most	much
no	some		

  There was *little applause*.
  He did not speak *much English*.
  We need *more information*.

⚠ BE CAREFUL

The following general determiners can never be used with uncountable nouns.

a	an	another	both
each	either	every	few
many	neither	several	

5 Most of the determiners are also pronouns, except 'the', 'a', 'an', 'every', 'no', and the possessives.

   I saw <u>several</u> in the woods last night.
   There is <u>enough</u> for all of us.
   Have you got <u>any</u> that I could borrow?

You use 'one' as a pronoun instead of 'a' or 'an', 'none' instead of 'no', and 'each' instead of 'every'.

   Have you got <u>one</u>?
   There are <u>none</u> left.
   <u>Each</u> has a separate box and number.

Unit 29: Main uses of 'the'

Main points

- You can use 'the' in front of any noun.
- You use 'the' when the person you are talking to knows which person or thing you mean.
- You use 'the' when you are referring back to someone or something.
- You use 'the' when you are specifying which person or thing you are talking about.
- You use 'the' when you are referring to something that is unique.
- You use 'the' when you want to use one thing as an example to say something about all things of the same type.

1 'The' is called the definite article, and is the commonest determiner. You use 'the' when the person you are talking to knows which person or thing you mean. You can use 'the' in front of any noun, whether it is a singular countable noun, an uncountable noun, or a plural countable noun.

  She dropped <u>the can</u>.

I remembered <u>the fun</u> I had with them last summer.
<u>The girls</u> were not at home.

---

2 You use 'the' with a noun when you are referring back to someone or something that has already been mentioned.

I called for <u>a waiter</u> ... ... <u>The waiter</u> brought our bill.
I have bought <u>a house</u> in Wales... ... <u>The house</u> is next to a farm.

---

3 You use 'the' with a noun and a qualifier, such as a prepositional phrase or a relative clause, when you are specifying which person or thing you are talking about.

I've no idea about <u>the geography of Great Britain</u>.
<u>The book that I recommended</u> now costs over twenty pounds.

---

4 You use 'the' with a noun when you are referring to something of which there is only one in the world.

They all sat in <u>the sun</u>.
We have landed men on <u>the moon</u>.
<u>The sky</u> was a brilliant blue.

You also use 'the' when you are referring to something of which there is only one in a particular place.

> *Mrs Robertson heard that <u>the supermarket</u>*
> *had been shut down.*
> *He works at <u>the university</u>.*

---

5 You can use 'the' with a singular countable noun when you want to make a general statement about all things of that type. For example, if you say 'The whale is the largest mammal in the world', you are talking about all whales, not one particular whale.

> <u>The computer</u> *allows us to deal with a lot of data very quickly.*
> *My father's favourite flower is <u>the rose</u>.*
> <u>The peacock</u> *is native to India.*

---

6 You can use 'the' with a singular countable noun when you are referring to a system or service. For example, you can use 'the phone' to refer to a telephone system and 'the bus' to refer to a bus service.

> *I don't like using <u>the phone</u>.*
> *How long does it take to get to London on <u>the train</u>?*
> *That evening she won ten pounds on <u>the lottery</u>.*

7 You can use 'the' with the name of a
   musical instrument when you are talking
   about someone playing, or being able to
   play, a particular kind of instrument.

   'You play <u>the guitar</u>, I see,' said Simon.
   I was playing <u>the piano</u> when he arrived.

Unit 30: Other uses of 'the'

Main points

- You do not normally use 'the' with proper nouns referring to people. You do use 'the' with many proper nouns referring to geographical places.
- You use 'the' with some adjectives to talk about groups of people.

---

1 You do not normally use 'the' with proper nouns that are people's names. However, if you are talking about a family, you can say 'the Browns'.

You use 'the' with some titles, such as 'the Queen of England', and with the names of some organizations, buildings, newspapers, and works of art.

... _the_ United Nations... ... _the_ Taj Mahal ...
... _the_ Times... ... _the_ Mona Lisa ...

---

2 You do use 'the' with some proper nouns referring to geographical places.

... _the_ Bay of Biscay... ... _the_ Suez Canal ...
... _the_ Arabian Gulf... ... _the_ Pacific Ocean ...

You use 'the' with countries whose names include words such as 'kingdom', 'republic', 'states', or 'union'.

> ... _the_ United Kingdom... ... _the_ Czech
> Republic ...

You use 'the' with countries that have
plural nouns as their names.

> ... _the_ Netherlands... ... _the_ Philippines ...

Note that you do not use 'the' with
countries that have singular nouns as
their names, such as 'Italy' or 'Turkey'.

You use 'the' with names of mountain
ranges and groups of islands.

> ... _the_ Alps... ... _the_ Himalayas ...
> ... _the_ Bahamas... ... _the_ Canaries ...

Note that you do not use 'the' with the
names of individual mountains such as
'Everest' or 'Etna', or the names of
individual islands such as 'Sicily', 'Minorca',
or 'Bali'.

You use 'the' with regions of the world, or
regions of a country that include 'north',
'south', 'east', or 'west'.

> ... _the_ Middle East... ... _the_ west of Ireland ...
> ... _the_ north of England... ... _the_ Far East ...

Note that there are some exceptions.

> ...North America... ...South-East Asia ...

You do not use 'the' with 'northern',
'southern', 'eastern', or 'western' and

a singular name.

> ... _northern_ England ... ... _western_ Africa ...

You use 'the' with the names of areas of water such as seas, oceans, rivers, canals, gulfs, and straits.

> .. _the_ Mediterranean Sea ...
> ... _the_ Atlantic Ocean ...
> ... _the_ river Ganges ...
> ... _the_ Panama Canal ...
> ... _the_ Gulf of Mexico ...
> ... _the_ straits of Gibraltar ...

Note that you do not use 'the' with lakes.

> ...Lake Geneva... ...Lake Superior ...

Note that you do not use 'the' with continents, cities, streets, or addresses.

> ...Asia ... ...Tokyo ... ...Oxford Street ...
> ...15 Park Street ...

---

3 You use 'the' with adjectives such as 'rich', 'poor', 'young', 'old', and 'unemployed' to talk about a general group of people. You do not need a noun.

> They were discussing the problem of _the unemployed_.

→ See Unit 19.

4 You use 'the' with some nationality adjectives to talk about the people who live in a country.

> *They will be increasingly dependent on the support of the French.*

With other nationalities, you use a plural noun.

> *...Germans ... ...the Americans...*

➔ See Unit 19.

5 You use 'the' with superlatives.

> *He was the cleverest man I ever knew.*
> *He was the youngest.*
> *His shoulders hurt the worst.*
> *It was the most exciting summer of their lives.*

Unit 31: 'A' and 'an'

Main points

- You only use 'a' or 'an' with singular countable nouns.
- You use 'a' or 'an' to talk about a person or thing for the first time.

1 You only use 'a' or 'an' with singular countable nouns. 'A' and 'an' are called the indefinite article.

> I got _a postcard_ from Susan.
> He was eating _an apple_.

Remember that you use 'a' in front of a word that begins with a consonant sound even if the first letter is a vowel, for example 'a piece, a university, a European language'. You use 'an' in front of a word that begins with a vowel sound even if the first letter is a consonant, for example 'an exercise, an idea, an honest man'.

---

2 You use 'a' or 'an' when you are talking about a person or thing for the first time.

> She picked up _a book_.
> After weeks of looking, we eventually bought _a house_.
> _A colleague_ and I carried out the research.

Note that the second time you refer to the same person or thing, you use 'the'.

> *She picked up _a book_ ... ... _The book_ was lying on the table.*
> *After weeks of looking, we bought _a house_ ... ... _The house_ was in a village.*

---

3 After the verb 'be' or another linking verb, you can use 'a' or 'an' with an adjective and a noun to give more information about someone or something.

> *His brother was _a sensitive child_.*
> *He seemed _a worried man_.*
> *It was _a really beautiful house_.*

You can also use 'a' or 'an' with a noun followed by a qualifier, such as a prepositional phrase or a relative clause, when you want to give more information about someone or something.

> *The information was contained in _an article on biology_.*
> *I chose _a picture that reminded me of my own country_.*

---

4 You use 'a' or 'an' after the verb 'be' or another linking verb when you are saying what someone is or what job they have.

> *He became _a school teacher_.*
> *She is _a model_ and _an artist_.*

5 You use 'a' or 'an' to mean 'one' with some numbers. You can use 'a' or 'an' with nouns that refer to whole numbers, fractions, money, weights, or measures.

a hundred	a quarter	a pound	a kilo
a thousand	a half	a dollar	a litre

6 You do not use 'a' or 'an' with uncountable nouns or plural countable nouns. You do not need to use a determiner at all with plural countable nouns, but you can use the determiners 'any', 'a few', 'many', 'several', or 'some'.

> I made <u>sandwiches</u> for lunch.
> There are <u>some sandwiches</u> in the fridge.
> Many adults don't listen to <u>children</u>.
> Do you have <u>any children</u>?

Note that if you do not use a determiner with a plural countable noun, you are often making a general statement about people or things of that type. For example, if you say 'I love parties', you mean all parties. However, if you say 'There are eggs in the kitchen', you mean there are some eggs. If you do use a determiner, you mean a number of people or things but not all of them, without saying exactly how many.

I have <u>some friends</u> coming for dinner.
He bought <u>some plants</u> for the house.
I have <u>some important things</u> to tell them.

Unit 32: All, most, no, none

Main points

- You use 'all' with plural countable nouns and uncountable nouns. You use 'all' to talk about every person or thing in the world, or in the group you are talking about.

- You use 'most' with plural countable nouns and uncountable nouns. You use 'most' to talk about nearly all of a number of people or things, or nearly all of a quantity of something.

- You use 'no' with singular and plural countable nouns and uncountable nouns. You use 'no' to say that something does not exist or is not present.

1 You use 'all' with plural countable nouns and uncountable nouns to talk about every person or thing in the world or in the group that you are talking about.

> _All children_ should complete the primary course.
> _All important decisions_ were taken by the government.
> He soon lost _all hope_ of becoming a rock star.
> _All luggage_ will be searched.

2 You use 'most' with plural countable nouns and uncountable nouns to talk about nearly all of a number of people or things, or nearly all of a quantity of something.

> *The method was suitable for <u>most purposes</u>.*
> *<u>Most good drivers</u> stop at zebra crossings.*
> *<u>Most milk</u> is bought in supermarkets.*
> *He ignored <u>most advice</u>, and did what he thought best.*

3 You use 'no' with singular countable nouns, plural countable nouns, and uncountable nouns to say that something does not exist or is not present.

> *There was <u>no chair</u> for me to sit on.*
> *They had <u>no immediate plans</u> to move house.*
> *<u>No money</u> was available for the operation.*

Note that if there is another word in the clause that makes it negative, you use 'any', not 'no'.

> *It has<u>n't</u> made <u>any difference</u>.*
> *He will <u>never</u> do <u>any work</u> for me again.*

4 'All' and 'most' are also pronouns, so you can say 'all of' and 'most of'. 'No' is not a pronoun, so you must say 'none of'.

> *He spent <u>all of the money</u> on a new car.*

Most of my friends live in London.
None of those farmers had ever driven a tractor.

Note that you use 'all of', 'most of', and 'none of' with an object pronoun.

All of us were sleeping.
I had seen *most of them* before.
None of them came to the party.

Note that if the clause is already negative, you use 'any of', not 'none of'.

I had<u>n't</u> eaten *any of* the biscuits.

When 'none of' is followed by a plural noun or pronoun, the verb is usually plural, but can be singular.

None of us are the same.
None of them has lasted very long.

5 You can use 'all the' with a plural countable noun or an uncountable noun. There is no difference in meaning between 'all the' and 'all of the'.

All the girls think it's great.
All the best jokes came at the end of the programme.
Thank you for *all the help* you gave me.

⚠ **BE CAREFUL**

You cannot say 'most the' or 'none the'. You must say 'most of the' or 'none of the'.

6 You can use 'all' after a noun or pronoun to emphasize that the noun or pronoun refers to everyone or everything that has been mentioned or is involved.

Note that you can use 'all' to emphasize the subject or the object.

> _The band all_ live together in the same house.
> I enjoyed _it all_.

Unit 33: Both, either, neither

Main points

- You use 'both', 'either', and 'neither' to talk about two people or things that have been mentioned or are known to the hearer.
- You use 'both' with plural nouns, and 'either' and 'neither' with singular nouns.
- You use 'both of', 'either of', and 'neither of' with plural nouns or pronouns.

1 You use 'both', 'either', and 'neither' when you are saying something about two people or things that have been mentioned, or are known to the person you are talking to.

> There were excellent performances from <u>both actresses</u>.
> Denis held his mug in <u>both hands</u>.
> No argument could move <u>either man</u> from this decision.
> <u>Neither report</u> mentioned the Americans.

2 You use 'both' when you think of the two people or things as a group. You use 'both' with a plural noun.

> *Both children were happy with their presents.*
> *Both policies make good sense.*

---

3 You use 'either' when you think of the two people or things as individuals. You use 'either' with a singular noun.

> *Either way is acceptable.*
> *She could not see either man.*

---

4 You use 'neither' when you are thinking of the two people or things as individuals and you are making a negative statement about them. You use 'neither' with a singular noun.

> *In reality, neither party was enthusiastic.*
> *Neither man knew what he was doing.*

---

5 You can use 'both' with a specific determiner such as 'the', 'these', or 'my'.

> *Both the young men agreed to come.*
> *Both these books have been recommended to us.*
> *Both her parents were dead.*

⚠ **BE CAREFUL**

You cannot use 'either' or 'neither' with a specific determiner.

6 You can use 'both of', 'either of', or 'neither of' with a plural noun or pronoun.

Note that when 'both of', 'either of', and 'neither of' are followed by a noun rather than a pronoun, you must use a specific determiner such as 'the', 'these', or 'her' before the noun.

> _Both of these restaurants_ are excellent.
> _Either of them_ could have done the job.
> _Neither of our boys_ was involved.

Note that 'neither of' is normally used with a singular verb but it can be used with a plural verb.

> _Neither of us <u>was having</u> any luck._
> _Neither of the children <u>were</u> there._

7 Remember that you can also use 'both', 'either', and 'neither' as conjunctions. You use 'both...and' to give two alternatives and say that each of them is possible or true.

> _I am looking for opportunities <u>both</u> in this country <u>and</u> abroad._
> _<u>Both</u> I <u>and</u> my wife were surprised to see you there._

You use 'either...or' to give two alternatives and say that only one of them is possible or true.

You can have <u>either</u> fruit <u>or</u> ice cream.
I was expecting you <u>either</u> today <u>or</u>
tomorrow.
You <u>either</u> love him <u>or</u> hate him.

You also use 'neither...nor' to give two
alternatives and say that each of them is
not possible or is not true.

<u>Neither</u> Margaret <u>nor</u> John was there.
He did it <u>neither</u> quickly <u>nor</u> well.

Unit 34: Quantity 1

Main points

- You use 'much' and 'little' with uncountable nouns to talk about a quantity of something.

- You use 'many' and 'few' with plural nouns to talk about a number of people or things.

- You use 'much' in negative sentences and questions, and 'a lot of' or 'plenty of' rather than 'much' in affirmative sentences.

- You use 'more' and 'less' with uncountable nouns, and 'more' and 'fewer' with plural countable nouns.

---

1 You use 'much' to talk about a large quantity of something, and 'little' to talk about a small quantity of something. You only use 'much' and 'little' with uncountable nouns.

   I haven't got <u>much time</u>.
   We've made <u>little progress</u>.

---

2 You use 'many' to talk about a large number of people or things, and 'few' to talk about a small number of people or things. You can only use 'many' and 'few'

with plural countable nouns.

> *He wrote <u>many novels</u>.*
> *There were <u>few visitors</u> to our house.*

3   You normally use 'much' in negative
    sentences and questions.

> *He did <u>not</u> speak <u>much</u> English.*
> *How <u>much</u> time do we have?*

In affirmative sentences you do not
usually use 'much'. You use 'a lot of',
'lots of', or 'plenty of' instead. You can use
them with both uncountable nouns and
plural nouns.

> *He demanded <u>a lot of attention</u>.*
> *I make <u>a lot of mistakes</u>.*
> *They spent <u>lots of time</u> on the project.*
> *It was a large room with <u>lots of windows</u>.*
> *I've got <u>plenty of money</u>.*
> *There are always <u>plenty of jobs</u> to be done.*

Note that you can use 'so much' and
'too much' in affirmative sentences.

> *She spends <u>so much time</u> here.*
> *There is <u>too much chance</u> of error.*

4   You use 'so much' and 'so many' to
    emphasize that a large quantity of
    something, or a large number of people or
    things, is involved.

I have <u>so much work</u> to do.
I love this shop – it has <u>so many</u>
<u>interesting books</u>.

You use 'too much' and 'too many' to say that the quantity of something, or the number of people or things, is larger than is reasonable or necessary.

He has <u>too much work</u>.
She has <u>too many toys</u>.

You use 'very many' to emphasize that a large number of people or things are involved.

<u>Very many elderly people</u> live alone.

Note that 'very much' is used with nouns and verbs.

There isn't <u>very much time</u>.
I <u>liked</u> it <u>very much</u>.

5 You use 'few' and 'little' to emphasize that only a small quantity of something or a small number of people or things are involved. They can be used with 'very' for greater emphasis.

The town has <u>few monuments</u>.
I have <u>little time</u> for anything but work.
<u>Very few cars</u> had reversing lights.
I had <u>very little money</u> left.

Note that 'a few' and 'a little' just indicate that a quantity or number is small.

He spread <u>a little honey</u> on a slice of bread.
I usually do <u>a few jobs</u> for him in the house.

---

6 You use 'more' with uncountable nouns and plural countable nouns to refer to a quantity of something or a number of people or things that is greater than another quantity or number.

His visit might do <u>more harm</u> than good.
He does <u>more hours</u> than I do.

You use 'less' with uncountable nouns to refer to an amount of something that is smaller than another amount.

The poor have <u>less access</u> to education.
This machinery uses <u>less energy</u>.

You use 'fewer', or 'less' in informal English, with plural nouns to refer to a number of people or things that is smaller than another number.

There are <u>fewer trees</u> here.
They have sold <u>less computers</u> this year.

Unit 35: Quantity 2

Main points

- You use 'some' to talk about a quantity or number without being precise.
- You use 'any' to talk about a quantity or number that may or may not exist.
- You use 'another', or 'another' and a number, to talk about additional people or things.
- You use 'each' and 'every' to talk about all the members of a group of people or things.

1 You use 'some' with uncountable nouns and plural nouns to talk about a quantity of something or a number of people or things without being precise.

> *I have left <u>some food</u> for you in the fridge.*
> *<u>Some trains</u> are running late.*

You normally use 'some' in affirmative sentences.

> *There's <u>some chocolate cake</u> over there.*
> *I had <u>some good ideas</u>.*

You use 'some' in questions when you expect the answer to be 'yes', for example in offers or requests.

> *Would you like <u>some coffee</u>?*

Could you give me some examples?

In informal English, you can use 'some' with a singular noun when you do not know which person or thing is involved, or you think it does not matter.

> *Some man phoned, but didn't leave his number.*
> *Is there some problem?*

---

2 You use 'any' in front of plural and uncountable nouns to talk about a quantity of something that may or may not exist. You normally use 'any' in questions and negative sentences.

> *Are there any jobs available?*
> *It hasn't made any difference.*

You use 'any' with a singular noun to emphasize that it does not matter which person or thing is involved.

> *Any container will do.*

You can use 'no' with an affirmative verb instead of 'not any'.

> *There weren't any tomatoes left.*
> *There were no tomatoes left.*

You can also use 'not' and 'any', or 'no', with a comparative.

> *Her house wasn't any better than ours.*
> *Her house was no better than ours.*

3 You use 'another' with singular nouns to talk about an additional person or thing.

> *Could I have <u>another cup of coffee</u>?*
> *He opened <u>another shop</u> last month.*

You can also use 'another' with a number and a plural noun to talk about more people or things.

> *<u>Another four years</u> passed before we met again.*
> *I've got <u>another three books</u> to read.*

You use 'other' with plural nouns and 'the other' with singular or plural nouns.

> *I've got <u>other things</u> to think about.*
> *<u>The other</u> man has gone.*
> *<u>The other</u> European countries have all beaten us.*

4 You use 'each' or 'every' with a singular noun to talk about all the members of a group of people or things. You use 'each' when you are thinking about the members as individuals, and 'every' when you are making a general statement about all of them.

> *<u>Each county</u> is subdivided into several districts.*
> *<u>Each applicant</u> has five choices.*
> *<u>Every child</u> had milk <u>every day</u>.*
> *She spoke to <u>every person</u> at that party.*

You can modify 'every' but not 'each'.

He spoke to them <u>nearly every day</u>.
We went out <u>almost every evening</u>.

---

5 You can use 'some of', 'any of', or 'each of', and a noun phrase to talk about a number of people or things in a group of people or things.

<u>Some of the information</u> has already been analysed.
It was more expensive than <u>any of the other magazines</u>.
He gave <u>each of us</u> advice about our present goals.

You can use 'each of' and a plural noun phrase, but 'every' must be followed by 'one of'.

<u>Each of the drawings</u> is different.
<u>Every one of them</u> is given a financial target.

Note that you can also use 'each' with 'one of'.

This view of poverty influences <u>each one of us</u>.

Unit 36: Position of adjectives

Main points

- There are two main positions for adjectives: in front of a noun, or as the complement of a linking verb.
- Most adjectives can be used in either of these positions, but some adjectives can only be used in one.

1 Most adjectives can be used in a noun phrase, after determiners and numbers if there are any, in front of the noun.

> He had a _beautiful smile_.
> She bought a loaf of _white bread_.
> Six _new episodes_ will be filmed.
> There was no _clear evidence_.

2 Most adjectives can also be used after a linking verb such as 'be', 'become', or 'feel'.

> I'_m cold_.
> I _felt angry_.
> Nobody _seemed amused_.

3 Some adjectives are normally used only after a linking verb.

afraid	alive	alone	asleep
awake	aware	content	due
glad	ill	ready	sorry
sure	unable	well	

For example, you can say 'She was glad',
but you do not talk about 'a glad woman'.

I wanted to <u>be alone</u>.
We were <u>getting ready</u> for bed.
I'<u>m</u> not quite <u>sure</u>.
He didn't know whether to <u>feel glad</u> or <u>sorry</u>.

---

4 Some adjectives are normally used only in
front of a noun.

atomic	countless	digital
east	eastern	existing
indoor	introductory	maximum
neighbouring	north	northern
occasional	outdoor	south
southern	west	western

For example, you talk about 'an atomic
bomb', but you do not say 'The bomb was
atomic'.

He sent <u>countless letters</u> to the newspapers.
This book includes a good <u>introductory</u>
<u>chapter</u> on forests.
He lives on the <u>west coast</u> of Scotland.

5 Emphasizing adjectives such as 'absolute' and 'utter' always comes in front of a noun.

> *Some of it was <u>absolute rubbish</u>.*
> *He made me feel like a <u>complete idiot</u>.*

→ See Unit 42 for information about emphasizing adjectives.

6 Some adjectives that describe size or age can come after a noun phrase consisting of a number or determiner and a noun that indicates the unit of measurement.

deep	high	long	old	tall	thick	wide

> *He was about <u>six feet tall</u>.*
> *The water was <u>several metres deep</u>.*
> *The baby is <u>nine months old</u>.*

Note that you do not say 'two pounds heavy'. You say 'two pounds in weight'.

7 A few adjectives are used alone after a noun.

designate	elect	galore	incarnate

> *She was now the <u>president elect</u>.*
> *There are empty <u>houses galore</u>.*

8 A few adjectives have a different meaning depending on whether they come in front of or after a noun.

concerned	involved	present
proper	responsible	

For example, 'the concerned mother' means a mother who is worried, but 'the mother concerned' means the mother who has been mentioned.

It's one of those incredibly <u>involved stories</u>.
The <u>people involved</u> are all doctors.
I'm worried about the <u>present situation</u>.
Of the 18 <u>people present</u>, I knew only one.
Her parents were trying to act in a <u>responsible manner</u>.
We do not know the <u>person responsible</u> for his death.

Unit 37: Order of adjectives

Main points

- You put opinion adjectives in front of descriptive adjectives.
- You put general opinion adjectives in front of specific opinion adjectives.
- You can sometimes vary the order of adjectives.
- If you use two or more descriptive adjectives, you put them in a particular order.
- If you use a noun in front of another noun, you put any adjectives in front of the first noun.

1 You often want to add more information to a noun than you can with one adjective. In theory, you can use the adjectives in any order, depending on the quality you want to emphasize. In practice, however, there is a normal order.

When you use two or more adjectives in front of a noun, you usually put an adjective that expresses your opinion in front of an adjective that just describes something.

You live in a <u>nice big</u> house.

He is a <u>naughty little</u> boy.
She was wearing a <u>beautiful pink</u> suit.

---

2   When you use more than one adjective to
   express your opinion, an adjective with a
   more general meaning such as 'good',
   'bad', 'nice', or 'lovely' usually comes before
   an adjective with a more specific meaning
   such as 'comfortable', 'clean', or 'dirty'.

   *I sat in a <u>lovely comfortable</u> armchair in
   the corner.*
   He put on a <u>nice clean</u> shirt.
   It was a <u>horrible dirty</u> room.

---

3   You can use adjectives to describe various
   qualities of people or things. For example,
   you might want to indicate their size, their
   shape, or the country they come from.

   Descriptive adjectives belong to six main
   types, but you are unlikely ever to use all
   six types in the same noun phrase. If you
   did, you would normally put them in the
   following order:

size	age	shape
colour	nationality	material

   This means that if you want to use an 'age'
   adjective and a 'nationality' adjective, you
   put the 'age' adjective first.

We met some <u>young Chinese</u> girls.

Similarly, a 'shape' adjective normally comes before a 'colour' adjective.

He had <u>round black</u> eyes.

Other combinations of adjectives follow the same order.

Note that 'material' means any substance, not only cloth.

There was a <u>large round wooden</u> table in the room.
The man was carrying a <u>small black plastic</u> bag.

---

4 You usually put comparative and superlative adjectives in front of other adjectives.

Some of the <u>better English</u> actors have gone to live in Hollywood.
These are the <u>highest monthly</u> figures on record.

---

5 When you use a noun in front of another noun, you never put adjectives between them. You put any adjectives in front of the first noun.

He works in the <u>French</u> film industry.
He receives a <u>large weekly</u> cash payment.

6 When you use two adjectives as the complement of a linking verb, you use a conjunction such as 'and' to link them. With three or more adjectives, you link the last two with a conjunction, and put commas after the others. You can also put a comma before the conjunction.

> *The day was <u>hot and dusty</u>.*
> *The room was <u>large but square</u>.*
> *The house was <u>old, damp and smelly</u>.*
> *We felt <u>hot, tired, and thirsty</u>.*

Unit 38: Adjective + 'to' or 'that'

Main points

- Adjectives used after linking verbs are often followed by 'to'-infinitive clauses or 'that'-clauses.
- Some adjectives are always followed by 'to'-infinitive clauses.
- You often use 'to'-infinitive clauses or 'that'-clauses after adjectives to express feelings or opinions.
- You often use 'to'-infinitive clauses after adjectives when the subject is impersonal 'it'.

1 After linking verbs, you often use adjectives that describe how someone feels about an action or situation. With some adjectives, you can add a 'to'-infinitive clause or a 'that'-clause to say what the action or situation is.

afraid	anxious	ashamed
disappointed	frightened	glad
happy	pleased	proud
sad	surprised	unhappy

If the subject is the same in both clauses, you usually use a 'to'-infinitive clause. If the subject is different, you must use a 'that'-clause.

I was <u>happy to see</u> them again.
He was <u>happy that</u> they were coming.

You often use a 'to'-infinitive clause when talking about future time in relation to the main clause.

I am <u>afraid to go</u> home.
He was <u>anxious to leave</u> before it got dark.

You often use a 'that'-clause when talking about present or past time in relation to the main clause.

He was <u>anxious that</u> the passport was missing.
They were <u>afraid that</u> I might have talked to the police.

2 You often use 'sorry' with a 'that'-clause. Note that 'that' is often omitted.

I'm very <u>sorry that</u> I can't join you.
I'm <u>sorry</u> I'm so late.

3 Some adjectives are not usually used alone, but have a 'to'-infinitive clause after them to say what action or situation the adjective relates to.

able	apt	bound	due
inclined	liable	likely	prepared
ready	unlikely	unwilling	willing

They were <u>unable to help</u> her.
They were not <u>likely to forget</u> it
I am <u>willing to try</u>.
I'm <u>prepared to say</u> I was wrong.

4 When you want to express an opinion about someone or something, you often use an adjective followed by a 'to'-infinitive clause.

| difficult | easy | impossible | possible |
| right | wrong | | |

She had been <u>easy to deceive</u>.
The windows will be almost <u>impossible to open</u>.
Am I <u>wrong to stay</u> here?

Note that in the first two examples, the subject of the main clause is the object of the 'to'-infinitive clause. In the third example, the subject is the same in both clauses.

5 With some adjectives, you use a 'that'-clause to express an opinion about someone or something.

awful	bad	essential	
extraordinary	funny	good	important
interesting	obvious	sad	true

> *I was <u>sad that</u> people had reacted in this way.*
> *It is <u>extraordinary that</u> we should ever have met!*

---

6 You can also use adjectives with 'to'-infinitive clauses after 'it' as the impersonal subject. You use the preposition 'of' or 'for' to indicate the person or thing that the adjective relates to.

> *It was <u>easy to find</u> the path.*
> *It was <u>good of John to help</u> me.*
> *It was <u>difficult for her to find</u> a job.*

→ See Unit 21 for 'it' as impersonal subject.

→ See Unit 55 for more information about adjectives followed by 'of' or 'for'.

Unit 39: Qualitative and classifying adjectives

Main points

- There are two main types of adjective: qualitative adjectives and classifying adjectives.

- Qualitative adjectives describe a quality that someone or something has, while classifying adjectives show the class that something belongs to.

- Qualitative adjectives are gradable: they have comparative and superlative forms, and they can be used with adverbs like 'very'. Classifying adjectives are not gradable.

---

1 Qualitative adjectives describe a quality that someone or something has, such as 'sad', 'pretty', 'small', 'wise', and 'interesting'.

> That was a _sad_ story.
> I think it would be _wise_ to give up.
> He had led an _interesting_ life.

2 Qualitative adjectives are gradable. This means that you can use adverbs like 'very' and 'rather' in front of them. They also have comparative forms, such as 'bigger' and 'more interesting', and superlative forms, such as 'the biggest' and 'the most interesting'.

> *This question is <u>very important</u>.*
> *Jamie is <u>the smallest</u> child in his class.*
> *She feels much <u>happier</u> now.*
> *It was obvious that Blakemore was a <u>most unusual</u> man.*
> *Leslie was the subject of some <u>rather cruel</u> jokes.*

3 Classifying adjectives identify the type or 'class' that something belongs to. For example, if you say 'financial help', you are using the adjective 'financial' to describe what type of help you are talking about.

> *Our <u>annual</u> report is published online.*
> *The country has faced many <u>social</u>, <u>economic</u> and <u>political</u> problems.*
> *I want you to be responsible for the <u>technical</u> aspects of the work.*
> *I have devoted this week's column to <u>vegetarian</u> recipes.*

4 Classifying adjectives are not gradable. They do not have comparative and superlative forms, and they are not normally used with adverbs like 'very' and 'rather'.

> *The country faces many <u>social</u> and <u>economic</u> problems.*
> *The company is Canada's largest exporter of <u>industrial</u> machinery.*

For example, you cannot say that a problem is 'very social', or 'more social' than another problem, and you cannot say machinery is 'very industrial', or 'more industrial' than other machinery.

5 Some adjectives can be either qualitative or classifying, depending on the meaning.

For example, in 'an emotional person', 'emotional' is a qualitative adjective meaning 'feeling or expressing strong emotions'. A person can be 'very emotional', or 'more emotional' than someone else.

> *She described herself as an <u>emotional</u> person.*
> *I'm a <u>fairly emotional</u> person.*
> *Everyone knows she is a <u>very emotional</u> person.*
> *I'm not <u>the most emotional</u> person in the world.*

However, in 'the emotional needs of children', 'emotional' is a classifying adjective meaning 'relating to a person's emotions'. It cannot be used with words like 'very' or 'rather', and it does not have a comparative or superlative form.

She has a good understanding of the <u>emotional</u> needs of children.

Unit 40: '-ing' and '-ed' adjectives

Main points

- Many adjectives ending in '-ing' describe the effect that something has on someone's feelings.
- Some adjectives ending in '-ing' describe a process or state that continues over a period of time.
- Many adjectives ending in '-ed' describe people's feelings.

1 You use many '-ing' adjectives to describe the effect that something has on your feelings, or on the feelings of people in general. For example, if you talk about 'a surprising number', you mean that the number surprises you.

alarming	amazing	annoying
astonishing	boring	charming
confusing	convincing	depressing
disappointing	embarrassing	exciting
frightening	interesting	shocking
surprising	terrifying	tiring
welcoming	worrying	

He lives in a <u>charming</u> house just outside the town.
She always has a warm <u>welcoming</u> smile.

Most '-ing' adjectives have a related transitive verb.

→ See Unit 58 for information on transitive verbs.

2 You use some '-ing' adjectives to describe something that continues over a period of time.

ageing	booming	decreasing	dying
existing	increasing	living	remaining

Britain is an <u>ageing</u> society.
<u>Increasing</u> prices are making food very expensive.

These adjectives have related intransitive verbs.

→ See Unit 58 for information on intransitive verbs.

3 Many '-ed' adjectives describe people's feelings. They have the same form as the '-ed' participle of a transitive verb and have a passive meaning. For example, 'a frightened person' is a person who has been frightened by something.

alarmed	amused	astonished	bored
delighted	depressed	disappointed	excited
frightened	interested	satisfied	shocked
surprised	tired	worried	

She looks <u>alarmed</u> about something.
A <u>bored</u> student complained to his teacher.

Note that the '-ed' participles of irregular verbs do not end in '-ed', but can be used as adjectives.

See pages 474–479 for a list of irregular '-ed' participles.

The bird had a <u>broken</u> wing.
His coat was dirty and <u>torn</u>.

---

4 Like other adjectives, '-ing' and '-ed' adjectives can be:

- used in front of a noun

  They still show <u>amazing</u> loyalty to their parents.
  This is the most <u>terrifying</u> tale ever written.
  I was thanked by the <u>satisfied</u> customer.
  The <u>worried</u> authorities cancelled the match.

- used after linking verbs

  It's <u>amazing</u> what they can do.
  The present situation is <u>terrifying</u>.
  He felt <u>satisfied</u> with all the work he had done.
  My husband was <u>worried</u>.

* modified by adverbials such as 'quite', 'really', and 'very'

The film was <u>quite boring</u>.
There is nothing <u>very surprising</u> in this.
She was <u>quite astonished</u> at his behaviour.
He was a <u>very disappointed</u> young man.

* used in the comparative and superlative

His argument was <u>more convincing</u> than mine.
He became even <u>more depressed</u> after she died.
This is one of <u>the most boring books</u> I've ever read.
She was <u>the most excited</u> child in the room.

5 A small number of '-ed' adjectives are mainly used after linking verbs such as 'be', 'become', or 'feel'. They are related to transitive verbs, and are often followed by a prepositional phrase, a 'to'-infinitive clause, or a 'that'-clause.

convinced	delighted	finished	interested
pleased	prepared	scared	thrilled
tired	touched		

The Brazilians are <u>pleased</u> with the results.
He was always <u>prepared</u> to account for his actions.
She was <u>scared</u> that they would find her.

Unit 41: Colour adjectives

Main points

- When you want to say what colour something is, you use a colour adjective such as 'blue' or 'orange'.

- You can use adjectives such as 'light', 'dark', and 'bright' in front of colour adjectives, to be more precise.

- You can use a colour adjective with '-ish' at the end, for example 'reddish', to describe a colour that does not have a precise name.

1 When you want to say what colour something is, you use a colour adjective.

> *Her eyes are <u>brown</u>.*
> *He sent a bunch of <u>red</u> roses and <u>white</u> lilies.*

2 If you want to be more precise about a colour, you use an adjective such as 'light', 'pale', 'dark', or 'bright', in front of a colour adjective.

> *He has <u>light brown</u> hair and <u>pale blue</u> eyes.*
> *The dress was <u>dark green</u>.*

Note that these words cannot be used with the colours 'black' or 'white', because

you cannot have different shades of black
and white.

---

3 If you want to talk about a colour that
does not have a definite name, you can
use a colour adjective with '-ish' added
to the end.

> *The plant has small <u>greenish</u> flowers.*
> *His teeth were chipped and <u>yellowish</u>.*

---

4 Colours can also be nouns.

> *The sky had turned to a deep <u>blue</u>.*
> *They sell colourful carpets in <u>reds</u>, <u>yellows</u>,*
> *and <u>purples</u>.*

Unit 42: Emphasizing adjectives

Main points

- Emphasizing adjectives are adjectives like 'absolute' and 'utter', which emphasize your feelings about someone or something.
- Emphasizing adjectives always come in front of a noun.
- 'Very' can also be used as an emphasizing adjective.

1 You can emphasize your feelings about something or someone by putting an emphasizing adjective in front of a noun. Here is a list of emphasizing adjectives:

absolute	complete	entire	outright
perfect	positive	pure	real
total	true	utter	

2 You can use an emphasizing adjective in front of a noun that refers to a person or thing, when the noun shows your opinion about them.

He made me feel like a <u>complete</u> idiot.
That book was <u>absolute</u> rubbish.

---

3 You can also use an emphasizing adjective in front of a noun that refers to an attitude or a strong emotion.

   She looked at him with <u>utter</u> contempt.
   The whole evening was <u>pure</u> bliss.

---

4 The word 'very' is sometimes used to emphasize a noun, in expressions like 'the very top' and 'the very end'.

   We reached the <u>very</u> top of the hill.
   Our house is at the <u>very</u> end of the street.

Unit 43: Comparison: basic forms

Main points

- You add '-er' for the comparative and '-est' for the superlative of one-syllable adjectives and adverbs.

- You use '-er' and '-est' with some two-syllable adjectives.

- You use 'more' for the comparative and 'most' for the superlative of most two-syllable adjectives, all longer adjectives, and adverbs ending in '-ly'.

- Some common adjectives and adverbs have irregular forms.

1 You add '-er' for the comparative form and '-est' for the superlative form of one-syllable adjectives and adverbs. If they end in '-e', you add '-r' and '-st'.

| cheap | → | cheaper | → | cheapest |
| safe | → | safer | → | safest |

close	cold	fast	hard	large
light	nice	poor	quick	rough
small	weak	wide	young	

They worked <u>harder</u>.
I've found a <u>nicer</u> hotel.

If they end in a single vowel and consonant (except '-w'), double the consonant.

big	→	bigger	→	biggest

fat	hot	sad	thin	wet

The day grew <u>hotter</u>.
Henry was the <u>biggest</u> of them.

2 With two-syllable adjectives and adverbs ending in a consonant and '-y', you change the '-y' to '-i' and add '-er' and '-est'.

happy	→	happier	→	happiest

busy	dirty	easy	funny
heavy	lovely	lucky	pretty
silly	steady	tiny	

It couldn't be <u>easier</u>.
That is the <u>funniest</u> bit of the film.

3 You use 'more' for the comparative and 'most' for the superlative of most two-syllable adjectives, all longer adjectives, and adverbs ending in '-ly'.

careful	→ more careful	→ most careful
beautiful	→ more beautiful	→ most beautiful
seriously	→ more seriously	→ most seriously

Be more careful next time.
They are the most beautiful gardens in the world.
It affected Clive most seriously.

Note that for 'early' as an adjective or adverb, you use 'earlier' and 'earliest', not 'more' and 'most'.

4 With some common two-syllable adjectives and adverbs you can either use 'more' and 'most', or add '-er' and '-est'. (Some of them end in -y, in which case you change the '-y' to '-i' and add '-er' and '-est'.)

angry	costly	cruel	friendly	gentle
narrow	remote	risky	shallow	stupid

Energy is becoming more costly.
It was the costliest disaster in history.

Note that 'clever' and 'quiet' only add '-er' and '-est'.

It was quieter outside.
He was the cleverest man I ever knew.

5 You normally use 'the' with superlative adjectives in front of a noun, but you can omit 'the' after a linking verb.

> It was <u>the happiest</u> day of my life.
> I was <u>happiest</u> when I was on my own.

⚠ BE CAREFUL

When 'most' is used without 'the' in front of adjectives and adverbs, it often means almost the same as 'very'.

> This book was <u>most interesting</u>.
> I object <u>most strongly</u>.

6 A few common adjectives and adverbs have irregular comparative and superlative forms.

```
good/well → better → best
bad/badly → worse → worst
far → farther → farthest
      further → furthest
old → older → oldest
      elder → eldest
```

> She wanted to know him <u>better</u>.
> She sat near the <u>furthest</u> window.

Note that you use 'elder' or 'eldest' to say which brother, sister, or child in a family you mean.

> Our <u>eldest</u> daughter couldn't come.

Unit 44: Comparison: uses

Main points

- Comparative adjectives are used to compare people or things.
- Superlative adjectives are used to say that one person or thing has more of a quality than others in a group or others of that kind.
- Comparative adverbs are used in the same way as comparative adjectives.

1 You use comparative adjectives to compare one person or thing with another, or with the same person or thing at another time. After a comparative adjective, you often use 'than'

> *She was much <u>older than</u> me.*
> *I am <u>happier than</u> I have ever been.*

2 You use a superlative to say that one person or thing has more of a quality than others in a group or others of that kind.

> *Tokyo is Japan's <u>largest city</u>.*
> *He was <u>the tallest person</u> there.*

3 You can use comparative and superlative adjectives in front of a noun.

> I was _a better writer_ than he was.
> He had _more important things_ to do.
> It was _the quickest route_ from Rome to Naples.

You can also use comparative and superlative adjectives after linking verbs.

> My brother is _younger_ than me.
> He feels _more content_ now.
> The sergeant was _the tallest_.
> This book was _the most interesting_.

4 You can use adverbs of degree in front of comparative adjectives.

a bit	a good deal	a great deal
a little	a lot	far
much	rather	slightly

> This car's _a bit more expensive_.
> Now I feel _a great deal more confident_.
> It's _a rather more complicated_ story than that.

You can also use adverbs of degree such as 'by far', 'easily', 'much', or 'quite' in front of 'the' and superlative adjectives.

> It was _by far the worst hospital_ I had ever seen.

She was <u>easily the most intelligent person</u> in the class.

Note that you can put 'very' between 'the' and a superlative adjective ending in '-est'.

It was of <u>the very highest quality</u>.

---

5 When you want to say that one situation depends on another, you can use 'the' and a comparative followed by 'the' and another comparative.

<u>The smaller</u> it is, <u>the cheaper</u> it is to post.
<u>The larger</u> the organisation is, <u>the greater</u> the problem of administration becomes.

When you want to say that something increases or decreases, you can use two comparatives linked by 'and'.

It's getting <u>harder and harder</u> to find a job.
Cars are becoming <u>more and more expensive</u>.

6 After a superlative adjective, you can use a prepositional phrase to specify the group you are talking about.

Henry was <u>the biggest of them</u>.
These cakes are probably <u>the best in the world</u>.
He was <u>the most dangerous man in the country</u>.

7 You use the same structures in comparisons using adverbs as those given for adjectives:

- 'than' after comparative adverbs

  Prices have been rising <u>faster than</u> incomes.

- 'the' and a comparative adverb followed by 'the' and another comparative adverb

  <u>The quicker</u> we finish, <u>the sooner</u> we will go home.

- two comparative adverbs linked by 'and'

  He sounded <u>worse and worse</u>.
  He drove <u>faster and faster</u> till we told him to stop.

Unit 45: Other ways of comparing

Main points

- This includes structures such as: 'as...as', 'the same (as)' and 'like'.
- You use 'as...as...' to compare people or things.
- You can also compare people or things by using 'the same (as)'.
- You can also compare people or things by using a linking verb and a phrase beginning with 'like'.

1 You use 'as...as...' to compare people or things that are similar in some way.

You use 'as' and an adjective or adverb, followed by 'as' and a noun phrase, an adverbial, or a clause.

> You're <u>as bad as your sister</u>.
> The airport was <u>as crowded as ever</u>.
> I am <u>as good as she is</u>.
> Let us examine it <u>as carefully as we can</u>.

2 You can make a negative comparison using 'not as...as...' or 'not so...as...'.

> The food was<u>n't as</u> good <u>as</u> yesterday.
> They are <u>not as</u> clever <u>as</u> they appear to be.

He is <u>not so</u> old <u>as</u> I thought.

---

3 You can use the adverbs 'almost', 'just', 'nearly', or 'quite' in front of 'as...as...'.

He was <u>almost as</u> fast <u>as</u> his brother.
Mary was <u>just as</u> pale <u>as</u> before.
She was <u>nearly as</u> tall <u>as</u> he was.

In a negative comparison, you can use 'not nearly' or 'not quite' before 'as...as...'.

This is <u>not nearly as</u> complicated <u>as</u> it sounds.
The hotel was <u>not quite as</u> good <u>as</u> they expected.

---

4 When you want to say that one thing is very similar to something else, you can use 'the same as' followed by a noun phrase, an adverbial, or a clause.

Your bag is <u>the same as</u> mine.
I said <u>the same as</u> always.
She looked <u>the same as</u> she did yesterday.

If people or things are very similar or identical, you can also say that they are 'the same'.

Teenage fashions are <u>the same</u> all over the world.
The initial stage of learning English is <u>the same</u> for many students.

You can use some adverbs in front of 'the same as' or 'the same'.

almost	exactly	just	more or less
much	nearly	roughly	virtually

He did <u>exactly the same as</u> John did.
You two look <u>almost the same</u>.

You can use 'the same' in front of a noun phrase, with or without 'as' after the noun phrase.

They reached almost <u>the same height</u>.
It was painted <u>the same colour as</u> the wall.

5 You can also compare people or things by using a linking verb such as 'be', 'feel', 'look', or 'seem' and a phrase beginning with 'like'.

It <u>was like</u> a dream.
He still <u>feels like</u> a child.
He <u>looked like</u> an actor.
The houses <u>seemed like</u> mansions.

You can use some adverbs in front of 'like'.

a bit	a little	exactly	just
least	less	more	most
quite	rather	somewhat	very

He looks <u>just like</u> a baby.

*Of all his children, she was the one <u>most
like</u> me.*

6 If the noun phrase after 'as' or 'like' in any
of these structures is a pronoun, you use
an object pronoun or possessive pronoun.

Jane was as clever as <u>him</u>.
His car is the same as <u>mine</u>.

7 You can also use 'less' and 'least' to make
comparisons with the opposite meaning
to 'more' and 'most'.

They were <u>less fortunate</u> than us.
He was <u>the least skilled</u> of the workers.
We see him <u>less frequently</u> than we used to.

Unit 46: Adverbials

Main points

- Adverbials are usually adverbs, adverb phrases, or prepositional phrases.
- Adverbials of manner, place, and time are used to say how, where, or when something happens.
- Adverbials usually come after the verb, or after the object if there is one.
- The usual order of adverbials is manner, then place, then time.

1 An adverbial is often one word, an adverb.

Sit there <u>quietly</u>, and listen to this music.
Come here <u>immediately</u>!

However, an adverbial can also be a group of words:

- an adverb phrase

  He did not play <u>well enough</u> to win.

- a prepositional phrase

  The children were playing <u>in the park</u>.

- a noun phrase, usually a time expression

  Come and see me <u>next week</u>.

2 You use an adverbial of manner to describe the way in which something happens or is done.

> They looked <u>anxiously</u> at each other.
> She listened <u>with great patience</u> as he told his story.

You use an adverbial of place to say where something happens.

> A plane flew <u>overhead</u>.
> No birds or animals came <u>near the body</u>.

You use an adverbial of time to say when something happens.

> She will be here <u>soon</u>.
> He was born <u>on 3 April 1925</u>.

3 You normally put adverbials of manner, place, and time after the main verb.

> She sang <u>beautifully</u>.
> The book was lying <u>on the table</u>.
> The car broke down <u>yesterday</u>.

If the verb has an object, you put the adverbial after the object.

> I did learn to play a few tunes <u>very badly</u>.
> Thomas made his decision <u>immediately</u>.
> He took the glasses <u>to the kitchen</u>.

If you are using more than one of these adverbials in a clause, the usual order is manner, then place, then time.

They were sitting *quite happily in the car*.
(manner, place)
She spoke *very well at the village hall
last night*. (manner, place, time)

---

4 You usually put adverbials of frequency,
probability, and duration in front of the
main verb.

She *occasionally comes* to my house.
You have *very probably heard* the news
by now.
They had *already given* me the money.

A few adverbs of degree also usually come
in front of the main verb.

She *really enjoyed* the party.

---

5 When you want to focus on an adverbial,
you can do this by putting it in a different
place in the clause:

- you can put an adverbial at the
  beginning of a clause, usually for
  emphasis

Slowly, he opened his eyes.
In September I travelled to California.
Next to the coffee machine stood a pile
of cups.

- Note that after adverbials of place, as in
  the last example, the verb can come in
  front of the subject.

- you can sometimes put adverbs and adverb phrases in front of the main verb for emphasis, but not prepositional phrases or noun phrases

  He <u>deliberately</u> chose it because it was cheap.
  I <u>very much</u> wanted to go with them.

- you can change the order of adverbials of manner, place, and time when you want to change the emphasis

  They were sitting <u>in the car quite happily</u>. (place, manner)
  <u>At the meeting last night</u>, she spoke <u>very well</u>. (place, time, manner)

Unit 47: Adverbials of manner

Main points

- Most adverbs of manner are formed by adding '-ly' to an adjective, but sometimes other spelling changes are needed.
- You cannot form adverbs from adjectives that end in '-ly'.
- Some adverbs have the same form as adjectives.
- You do not use adverbs after linking verbs; you use adjectives.
- Adverbials of manner are sometimes prepositional phrases or noun phrases.

---

1 Adverbs of manner are often formed by adding '-ly' to an adjective.

Adjectives:	bad beautiful careful quick quiet soft
Adverbs:	badly beautifully carefully quickly quietly softly

---

2 Adverbs formed in this way usually have a similar meaning to the adjective.

  She is as clever as she is <u>beautiful</u>.

He talked so politely and danced so <u>beautifully</u>.
'We must not talk. We must be <u>quiet</u>,' said Sita.
She wanted to sit <u>quietly</u>, to relax.

---

3 There are sometimes changes in spelling when an adverb is formed from an adjective.

'-le' changes to '-ly': gentle → gently
'-y' changes to '-ily': easy → easily
'-ic' changes to '-ically': automatic → automatically
'-ue' changes to '-uly': true → truly
'-ll' changes to '-lly': full → fully

Note that 'public' changes to 'publicly'.

⚠ **BE CAREFUL**

You cannot form adverbs from adjectives that already end in '-ly'. For example, you cannot form an adverb from the adjectives 'friendly', 'lovely', or 'likely'. You can sometimes use a prepositional phrase instead, for example 'in a friendly way'.

---

4 Some adverbs of manner have the same form as adjectives and have similar meanings, for example 'fast', 'hard', and 'late'.

I've always been interested in <u>fast</u> cars.
(adjective)
He was driving too <u>fast</u>. (adverb)

Note that 'hardly' and 'lately' are not adverbs of manner and have different meanings from the adjectives 'hard' and 'late'.

It was a <u>hard</u> decision to make.
I <u>hardly</u> had any time to talk to her.
The train was <u>late</u> as usual.
Have you seen John <u>lately</u>?

5 The adverb of manner related to the adjective 'good' is 'well'.

He is a <u>good</u> dancer.
He dances <u>well</u>.

Note that 'well' can sometimes be an adjective when it refers to someone's health.

'How are you?' – 'I am very <u>well</u>, thank you.'

6 You do not use adverbs after linking verbs such as 'be', 'become', 'feel', 'get', 'look', and 'seem'. You use an adjective after these verbs. For example, you do not say 'Sue felt happily'. You say 'Sue felt happy'.
→ See Unit 62 for more information on linking verbs.

7 You do not often use prepositional phrases or noun phrases as adverbials of manner. However, you occasionally need to use them, for example when there is no adverb form available. The prepositional phrases and noun phrases usually include a noun such as 'way', 'fashion', or 'manner', or a noun that refers to someone's voice.

> *She asked me <u>in such a nice manner</u> that I couldn't refuse.*
> *He did it <u>the right way</u>.*
> *They spoke <u>in angry tones</u>.*

Prepositional phrases with 'like' are also used as adverbials of manner.

> *I slept <u>like a baby</u>.*
> *He drove <u>like a madman</u>.*

Unit 48: Adverbials of time

Main points

- Adverbials of time can be time expressions such as 'last night'.
- Adverbials of time can be prepositional phrases with 'at', 'in', or 'on'.
- 'For' refers to a period of time in the past, present, or future.
- 'Since' refers to a point of time in the past.

1 You use adverbials of time to say when something happens. You often use noun phrases called 'time expressions' as adverbials of time.

yesterday	today		tomorrow last night
last year	next Saturday	next week	
the day after tomorrow		the other day	

Note that you do not use the prepositions 'at', 'in', or 'on' with time expressions.

One of my children wrote to me <u>today</u>.
So, you're coming back <u>next week</u>?

You often use time expressions with verbs in the present tense to talk about the future.

The plane leaves <u>tomorrow morning</u>.
They're coming <u>next week</u>.

---

2 You can use prepositional phrases as
adverbials of time:

● 'at' is used with:

clock times:	at eight o'clock, at three fifteen
religious festivals:	at Christmas, at Easter
mealtimes:	at breakfast, at lunchtimes
specific periods:	at night, at the weekend, at weekends, at half-term

● 'in' is used with:

seasons:	in autumn, in the spring
years and centuries:	in 1985, in the year 2000, in the nineteenth century
months:	in July, in December
parts of the day:	in the morning, in the evenings

● Note that you also use 'in' to say that
something will happen during or after a
period of time in the future.

I think we'll find out <u>in</u> the next few days.

● Note that you say 'in the morning', 'in
the afternoon', and 'in the evening', but
you say 'at night'.

• 'on' is used with:

days:	on Monday, on Tuesday morning, on Sunday evenings
special days:	on Christmas Day, on my birthday, on his wedding anniversary
dates:	on the twentieth of July, on June 21st

3 You use 'for' with verbs in any tense to say how long something continues to happen.

> He _is_ in Italy _for_ a month.
> I _remained_ silent _for_ a long time.

⚠ **BE CAREFUL**

You do not use 'during' to say how long something continues to happen. You cannot say 'I went there during three weeks'.

4 You use 'since' with a verb in the present perfect or past perfect to say when something started to happen.

> Marilyn _has lived_ in Paris _since_ 1984.
> I _had eaten_ nothing _since_ breakfast.

5 You can use many other prepositional phrases as adverbials of time. You use:

• 'during' and 'over' for a period of time in which something happens

> I saw him twice _during_ the holidays.

Will you stay here <u>over</u> Christmas?

- 'from...to/till/until' and 'between...and' for the beginning and end of a period of time

The building is closed <u>from</u> April <u>to</u> May.
She worked <u>from</u> four o'clock <u>till</u> ten o'clock.
Can you take the test <u>between</u> now <u>and</u> June?

- 'by' when you mean 'not later than'

<u>By</u> eleven o'clock, Brody was back in his office.
Can we get this finished <u>by</u> tomorrow?

- 'before' and 'after'

I saw him <u>before</u> the match.
She left the house <u>after</u> ten o'clock.

'Since', 'till', 'until', 'after', and 'before' can also be conjunctions with time clauses.
➔ See Unit 104.

I've been wearing glasses <u>since I was three</u>.

6 You use the adverb 'ago' with the past simple to say how long before the time of speaking something happened. You always put 'ago' after the period of time.

We saw him about a month <u>ago</u>.
John's wife died five years <u>ago</u>.

⚠ **BE CAREFUL**

You do not use 'ago' with the present perfect. You cannot say 'We have gone to Spain two years ago'.

Unit 49: Frequency and probability

Main points

- This includes words like: 'always', 'ever', 'never', 'perhaps', 'possibly' and 'probably'.
- Adverbials of frequency are used to say how often something happens.
- Adverbials of probability are used to say how sure you are about something.
- These adverbials usually come before the main verb, but they come after 'be' as a main verb.

1 You use adverbials of frequency to say how often something happens.

a lot	always	ever	frequently
hardly ever	never	normally	occasionally
often	rarely	seldom	sometimes
usually			

We <u>often</u> swam in the sea.
She <u>never</u> comes to my parties.
You must have noticed how tired he <u>sometimes</u> looks.

2 You use adverbials of probability to say
how sure you are about something.

certainly	definitely	maybe	obviously
perhaps	possibly	probably	really

I _definitely_ saw her yesterday.
The driver _probably_ knows the quickest and
best route.
Maybe he sincerely wanted to help his
country.

3 You usually put adverbials of frequency
and probability before the main verb and
after an auxiliary or a modal.

He _sometimes works_ downstairs in
the kitchen.
You _are definitely wasting_ your time.
I _have never had_ such a horrible meal!
I _shall never forget_ this day.
You _should obviously ask_ for a full
explanation.

Note that you usually put them after 'be'
as a main verb.

He _is always_ careful with his money.
You _are probably_ right.
Today's inflation figure _is certainly_ much too
high.

'Perhaps' usually comes at the beginning
of the sentence.

Perhaps the beaches are cleaner in the north.
Perhaps you need a current membership
card to get in.

'A lot' always comes after the main verb.

I go swimming <u>a lot</u> in the summer.
I have to travel <u>a lot</u> in my job.
We talked <u>a lot</u> about what we wanted to do.

---

4 'Never' is a negative adverb.

She <u>never</u> goes abroad.
I've <u>never</u> been to Europe.
*She <u>never</u> said anything about what
happened to her.*

You normally use 'ever' in questions,
negative sentences, and 'if'-clauses.

Have you <u>ever</u> been to a football match?
Don't <u>ever</u> do that again!
If you <u>ever</u> need anything, just call me.

Note that you can sometimes use 'ever'
in affirmative sentences, for example after
a superlative.

She is the <u>best</u> dancer I have <u>ever</u> seen.
That's the funniest thing I <u>ever</u> heard!
*This is the <u>most awful</u> evening I can <u>ever</u>
remember.*

You use 'hardly ever' in affirmative
sentences to mean almost never.

> *We <u>hardly ever</u> meet.*
> *We ate chips every night, but <u>hardly ever</u>
> had fish.*
> *There are so many great plays that are
> <u>hardly ever</u> performed.*

Unit 50: Adverbials of duration

Main points

- 'Already' is used to say that something has happened earlier than expected.
- 'Still' is used to say that something continues to happen until a particular time.
- 'Yet' is used to say that something has not happened before a particular time.
- 'Any longer', 'any more', 'no longer', and 'no more' are used to say that something has stopped happening.

1 You use adverbials of duration to say that an event or situation is continuing, stopping, or is not happening at the moment.

> She _still_ lives in London.
> I couldn't stand it _any more_.
> It isn't dark _yet_.

2 You use 'already' to say that something has happened sooner than it was expected to happen. You put 'already' in front of the main verb.

He had <u>already bought</u> the cups and saucers.
I've <u>already seen</u> them.
The guests were <u>already coming</u> in.

You put 'already' after 'be' as a main verb.

Julie was <u>already</u> in bed.

You can also use 'already' to emphasize that something is the case, for example when someone else does not know or is not sure.

I am <u>already</u> aware of that problem.

You do not normally use 'already' in negative statements, but you can use it in negative 'if'-clauses.

Show it to him <u>if he hasn't already seen it</u>.

You can put 'already' at the beginning or end of a clause for emphasis.

<u>Already</u> he was calculating the profit he could make.
I've done it <u>already</u>.

---

3   You use 'still' to say that a situation continues to exist up to a particular time in the past, present, or future. You put 'still' in front of the main verb.

We <u>were still waiting</u> for the election results.
My family <u>still lives</u> in India.
You <u>will still get</u> tickets, if you hurry.

Adverbials of duration

You put 'still' after 'be' as a main verb.

Martin's mother died, but his father <u>is still</u> alive.

You can use 'still' after the subject and before the verb phrase in negative sentences to express surprise or impatience.

You <u>still</u> haven't given us the keys.
He <u>still</u> didn't say a word.
It was after midnight, and he <u>still</u> wouldn't leave.

Remember that you can use 'still' at the beginning of a clause with a similar meaning to 'after all' or 'nevertheless'.

<u>Still</u>, he is my brother, so I'll have to help him.
<u>Still</u>, it's not too bad. We didn't lose all the money.

---

4 You use 'yet' at the end of negative sentences and questions to say that something has not happened or had not happened up to a particular time, but is or was expected to happen later.

We haven't got the tickets <u>yet</u>.
Have you joined the swimming club <u>yet</u>?
They hadn't seen the baby <u>yet</u>.

Remember that 'yet' can also be used at the beginning of a clause with a similar meaning to 'but'.

I don't miss her, <u>yet</u> I do often wonder where she went.
They know they won't win. <u>Yet</u> they keep on trying.

---

5 You use 'any longer' and 'any more' at the end of negative clauses to say that a past situation has ended and does not exist now or will not exist in the future.

I wanted the job, but I couldn't wait <u>any longer</u>.
He's not going to play <u>any more</u>.

In formal English, you can use an affirmative clause with 'no longer' and 'no more'. You can put them at the end of the clause, or in front of the main verb.

He could stand the pain <u>no more</u>.
He <u>no longer</u> wanted to buy it.

Unit 51: Adverbials of degree

Main points

- Adverbials of degree usually modify verbs.
- Some adverbials of degree can modify adjectives, other adverbs, or clauses.

1 You use adverbials of degree to modify verbs. They make the verb stronger or weaker.

> I <u>totally disagree</u>.
> I can <u>nearly swim</u>.

2 Some adverbs can come in front of a main verb, after a main verb, or after the object if there is one.

| badly | completely | greatly |
| seriously | strongly | totally |

> Mr Brooke <u>strongly</u> criticized them.
> I disagree <u>completely</u> with John Taylor.
> That argument doesn't convince me <u>totally</u>.

Some adverbs are mostly used in front of the verb.

| almost | largely | nearly | really | quite |

He <u>almost</u> crashed into a lorry.

Note that 'really' is used at the beginning of a clause to express surprise, and at the end of a clause as an adverb of manner.

<u>Really</u>, I didn't know that!
He wanted it <u>really</u>, but was too shy to ask.

'A lot' and 'very much' come after the main verb if there is no object, or after the object.

She helped <u>a lot</u>.
We liked him <u>very much</u>.

'Very much' can come after the subject and in front of verbs like 'want', 'prefer', and 'enjoy'.

I <u>very much</u> wanted to take it with me.

3 Some adverbs of degree go in front of adjectives or other adverbs and modify them.

awfully	extremely	fairly	pretty
quite	rather	really	very

...a <u>fairly large</u> office, with filing space.

Note that you can use 'rather' before or after 'a' or 'an' followed by an adjective and a noun.

Seaford is <u>rather a</u> pleasant town.
It is <u>a rather</u> complicated story.

When 'quite' means 'fairly', you put it in front of 'a' or 'an' followed by an adjective and a noun.

Joe gave me <u>quite a large sum</u> of money.

However, when 'quite' means 'extremely', you can put it after 'a'. You can say 'a quite enormous sum'.

---

4 You use some adverbs of degree to modify clauses and prepositional phrases.

entirely	just	largely	mainly
partly	simply		

Are you saying that <u>simply because I am here</u>?
I don't think it's worth going <u>just for a day</u>.

---

5 You use 'so' and 'such' to emphasize a quality that someone or something has. 'So' can be followed by an adjective, an adverb, or a noun phrase beginning with 'many', 'much', 'few', or 'little'.

John is <u>so interesting</u> to talk to.
Science is changing <u>so rapidly</u>.
I want to do <u>so many</u> different things.

'Such' is followed by a singular noun phrase with 'a', or a plural noun phrase.

There was <u>such a noise</u> we couldn't hear.
They said <u>such nasty things</u>.

⚠ **BE CAREFUL**

'So' is never followed by a singular noun phrase with 'a' or a plural noun phrase.

---

6 You use 'too' when you mean 'more than is necessary' or 'more than is good'. You can use 'too' before adjectives and adverbs, and before 'many', 'much', 'few', or 'little'.

The prices are <u>too high</u>.
I've been paying <u>too much</u> tax.

You use 'enough' after adjectives and adverbs.

I waited until my daughter was <u>old enough</u> to read.
He didn't work <u>quickly enough</u>.

Note that 'enough' is also a determiner.

We've got <u>enough money</u> to buy that car now.

---

7 You use emphasizing adverbs to modify adjectives such as 'astonishing', 'furious', and 'wonderful', which express extreme qualities.

absolutely	completely	entirely	perfectly
purely	quite	really	simply
totally	utterly		

I think he's <u>absolutely wonderful</u>.

Unit 52: Place and direction

Main points

- This includes words like: 'above', 'below', 'down', 'from', 'to', 'towards' and 'up'.
- You normally use prepositional phrases to say where a person or thing is, or the direction they are moving in.
- You can also use adverbs and adverb phrases for place and direction.
- Many words are both prepositions and adverbs.

1 You use prepositions to talk about the place where someone or something is. Prepositions are always followed by a noun phrase, which is called the object of the preposition.

above	among	at	behind
below	beneath	beside	between
in	inside	near	on
opposite	outside	over	round
through	under	underneath	

He stood <u>near</u> the door.
Two minutes later we were safely <u>inside</u> the taxi.

Two young people sat <u>opposite</u> me.

Note that some prepositions consist of more than one word.

| in between | in front of | next to | on top of |

There was a man standing <u>in front of</u> me.
She sat down <u>next to</u> him on the sofa.
The books were piled <u>on top of</u> each other.

2 You can also use prepositions to talk about the direction that someone or something is moving in, or the place that someone or something is moving towards.

across	along	back to	down	into
onto	out of	past	round	
through	to	towards	up	

He watched Karl run <u>across</u> the street.
They dived <u>into</u> the water.
She turned and rushed <u>out of</u> the room.

3 Many prepositions can be used both for place and direction.

The bank is just <u>across</u> the High Street.
(place)
I walked <u>across</u> the room. (direction)
We live in the big old house <u>over</u> the road.
(place)

I stole his keys and escaped <u>over</u> the wall.
(direction)

4 You can also use adverbs and adverb phrases for place and direction.

abroad	away	downstairs
downwards	here	indoors
outdoors	there	underground
upstairs	anywhere	everywhere
nowhere	somewhere	

Sheila was <u>here</u> a moment ago.
We could have walked <u>there</u> in an hour or so.
Can't you go <u>upstairs</u> and turn the bedroom light off?

Note that a few noun phrases can also be used as adverbials of place or direction.

Steve lives <u>next door</u> at number 23.
I thought we went <u>the other way</u> last time we came.

5 Many words can be used as prepositions and as adverbs, with no difference in meaning. Remember that prepositions have noun phrases as objects, but adverbs do not.

Did he fall <u>down the stairs</u>?
Please do sit <u>down</u>.

I looked <u>underneath the bed</u>, but the box had gone!
Always put a sheet of paper <u>underneath</u>.

Unit 53: Place – 'at', 'in', 'on'

Main points

- You use 'at' to talk about a place as a point.
- You use 'in' to talk about a place as an area.
- You use 'on' to talk about a place as a surface.

1 You use 'at' when you are thinking of a place as a point in space.

> She waited <u>at the bus stop</u> for over twenty minutes.
> 'Where were you last night?' – '<u>At Mick's house</u>.'

2 You also use 'at' with words such as 'back', 'bottom', 'end', 'front', and 'top' to talk about the different parts of a place.

> Mrs Castle was waiting <u>at the bottom</u> of the stairs.
> They escaped by a window <u>at the back</u> of the house.
> I saw a taxi <u>at the end</u> of the street.

You use 'at' with public places and institutions. Note that you also say 'at home' and 'at work'.

> *I have to be <u>at the station</u> by ten o'clock.*
> *We landed <u>at a small airport</u>.*
> *A friend of mine is <u>at Training College</u>.*
> *She wanted to stay <u>at home</u>.*

You say 'at the corner' or 'on the corner' when you are talking about streets.

> *The car was parked <u>at the corner</u> of the street.*
> *There's a telephone box <u>on the corner</u>.*

You say 'in the corner' when you are talking about a room.

> *She put the chair <u>in the corner</u> of the room.*

3 You use 'in' when you are talking about a place as an area. You use 'in' with:

- a country or geographical region

> *When I was <u>in Spain</u>, it was terribly cold.*
> *A thousand homes <u>in the east of Scotland</u> suffered power cuts.*

- a city, town, or village

> *I've been teaching at a college <u>in London</u>.*

- a building when you are talking about people or things inside it

> *They were sitting having dinner <u>in the restaurant</u>.*

You also use 'in' with containers of any kind when talking about things inside them.

She kept the cards <u>in a little box</u>.

---

4 Compare the use of 'at' and 'in' in these examples.

I had a hard day <u>at the office</u>.
('at' emphasizes the office as a public place or institution)
I left my coat behind <u>in the office</u>.
('in' emphasizes the office as a building)
There's a good film <u>at the cinema</u>.
('at' emphasizes the cinema as a public place)
It was very cold <u>in the cinema</u>.
('in' emphasizes the cinema as a building.)

---

5 When talking about addresses, you use 'at' when you give the house number, and 'in' when you just give the name of the street.

They used to live <u>at 5, Weston Road</u>.
She got a job <u>in Oxford Street</u>.

You use 'at' when you are talking about someone's house.

I'll see you <u>at Fred's house</u>.

6 You use 'on' when you are talking about a place as a surface. You can also use 'on top of'.

> *I sat down <u>on the sofa</u>.*
> *She put her keys <u>on top of the television</u>.*

You also use 'on' when you are thinking of a place as a point on a line, such as a road, a railway line, a river, or a coastline.

> *Scrabster is <u>on the north coast</u>.*
> *Oxford is <u>on the A34</u> between Birmingham and London.*

→ See Unit 48 for information on 'at', 'in', and 'on' in adverbials of time.

Unit 54: Transport prepositions

Main points

- This includes phrases like: 'by bus', 'in a car', 'on the plane', and 'off the train'.
- You can use 'by' with most forms of transport.
- You use 'in', 'into', and 'out of' with cars.
- You normally use 'on', 'onto', and 'off' with other forms of transport.

1 When you talk about the type of vehicle or transport you use to travel somewhere, you use 'by'.

by bus	by bicycle	by car	by coach
by plane	by train		

She had come <u>by car</u> with her husband.
I went <u>by bus and train</u> to Nottingham.

⚠ BE CAREFUL

If you want to say you walk somewhere, you say you go 'on foot', not 'by foot'.

Marie decided to continue <u>on foot</u>.

---

2 You use 'in', 'into', and 'out of' when you are talking about cars, vans, lorries, taxis, and ambulances.

> I followed them <u>in my car</u>.
> Mr Ward happened to be getting <u>into his lorry</u>.
> She was carried <u>out of the ambulance</u> and up the steps.

---

3 You use 'on', 'onto', and 'off' when you are talking about other forms of transport, such as buses, coaches, trains, ships, and planes.

> He was already <u>on the plane</u> from California.
> The last thing he wanted was to spend ten days <u>on a boat</u> with Hooper.
> He jumped back <u>onto the old bus</u>.
> Mr Bixby stepped <u>off the train</u> and walked quickly to the exit.

You can use 'in', 'into', and 'out of' with these other forms of transport, usually when you are focusing on the physical position or movement of the person, rather than stating what form of transport they are using.

> The passengers <u>in the plane</u> were beginning to panic.
> He got back <u>into the train</u> quickly, before Brian could stop him.
> We jumped <u>out of the bus</u> and ran into the nearest shop.

Unit 55: Adjective + preposition

Main points

- Some adjectives used after linking verbs can be used alone or followed by a prepositional phrase.

- Some adjectives must be followed by particular prepositions.

- Some adjectives can be followed by different prepositions to introduce different types of information.

1 When you use an adjective after a linking verb, you can often use the adjective on its own or followed by a prepositional phrase.
→ See Unit 38.

He was <u>afraid</u>.
He was <u>afraid of</u> his enemies.

2 Some adjectives cannot be used alone after a linking verb. If they are followed by a prepositional phrase, it must have a particular preposition:

aware of	accustomed to	unaware of
unaccustomed to	fond of	used to

I was <u>aware</u> of a police car behind me.
I've always been terribly <u>fond of</u> you.
He is <u>unaccustomed to</u> the heat.

---

3   Some adjectives can be used alone, or
    followed by a particular preposition:

- used alone, or with 'of' to specify the
  cause of a feeling

afraid	ashamed	convinced	critical
envious	frightened	jealous	proud
scared	suspicious	terrified	tired

They may feel <u>jealous of</u> your success.
I was <u>terrified of</u> her.
Jack was <u>proud of</u> his children.

- used alone, or with 'of' to specify the
  person who has a quality

brave	careless	clever	generous
good	intelligent	kind	nice
polite	sensible	silly	stupid
thoughtful	unkind	unreasonable	
wrong			

That was <u>clever of</u> you!
I turned the job in New York down, which
was <u>stupid of</u> me.
It was <u>generous of</u> him to accept my apology.

- used alone or used with 'to', usually referring to:

similarity:	close equal identical related similar
marriage:	married engaged
loyalty:	dedicated devoted loyal
rank:	junior senior

My problems are very <u>similar to</u> yours.
He was <u>dedicated to</u> his job.

- used alone, or followed by 'with' to specify the cause of a feeling

bored	content	displeased	dissatisfied
impatient	impressed	pleased	satisfied

I could never be <u>bored with</u> football.
He was <u>pleased with</u> her.

- used alone, or with 'at', usually referring to:

strong reactions:	alarmed amazed astonished shocked surprised
ability:	bad excellent good hopeless useless

He was <u>shocked at</u> the news.
She had always been <u>good at</u> languages.

- used alone, or with 'for' to specify the person or thing that a quality relates to

common	difficult	easy	essential
important	necessary	possible	
unnecessary	unusual	usual	

It's <u>difficult for young people</u> on their own.
It was <u>unusual for them</u> to go away at the weekend.

---

4 Some adjectives can be used alone, or used with different prepositions.

- used alone, with an impersonal subject and 'of' and the subject of the action, or with a personal subject and 'to' and the object of the action

cruel	friendly	generous	good
kind	mean	nasty	nice
polite	rude	unfriendly	unkind

It was <u>rude of</u> him to leave so suddenly.
She was <u>rude to</u> him for no reason.

- used alone, with 'about' to specify a thing or 'with' to specify a person

| angry | annoyed | delighted | disappointed |
| fed up | furious | happy | upset |

She was still <u>angry about</u> the result.
They're getting pretty <u>fed up with</u> him.

Unit 56: Noun + preposition

Main points

- 'Of' can be used to add many different types of information. 'With' is used to specify a quality or possession.

- Some nouns are always followed by particular prepositions.

---

1 You can give more information about a noun by adding a prepositional phrase after it.

> Four men _on holiday_ were in the car.
> A sound _behind him_ made him turn.

---

2 You often use the preposition 'of' after a noun to add various kinds of information. For example, you can use 'of' to indicate:

- what something is made of or consists of

> ...a wall _of stone_.
> A feeling _of panic_ was rising in him.

- what the subject matter of speech, writing, or a picture is

> She gave a brief account _of her interview_.
> There was a picture _of them both_ in the paper.

- what a person or thing belongs to or is connected with

  She was the daughter <u>of the village priest</u>.
  The boys sat on the floor <u>of the living room</u>.

- what qualities a person or thing has

  She was a woman <u>of energy and ambition</u>.
  They faced problems <u>of great complexity</u>.

3 After nouns referring to actions, you use 'of' to indicate the subject or object of the action.

> *...the arrival <u>of the police</u>.*
> *...the destruction <u>of their city</u>.*

After nouns referring to people who perform an action, you use 'of' to say what the action involves or is aimed at.

> *...supporters <u>of the hunger strike</u>.*
> *...a student <u>of English</u>.*

Note that you often use two nouns, rather than a noun and a prepositional phrase. For example, you say 'bank robbers', not 'robbers of the bank'.

4 After nouns referring to measurement, you use 'of' to give the exact figure.

> *...an average temperature <u>of 20 degrees</u>.*
> *...a speed <u>of 25 kilometres an hour</u>.*

You can use 'of' after a noun to give someone's age.

> *Jonathan was a child <u>of seven</u> when it happened.*

---

5 You use 'with' after a noun to say that a person or thing has a particular quality, feature, or possession.

> *...a girl <u>with red hair</u>.*
> *...the man <u>with the gun</u>.*

Note that you use 'in' after a noun to say what someone is wearing.

> *...a grey-haired man <u>in a raincoat</u>.*
> *...the man <u>in dark glasses</u>.*

---

6 Some nouns are usually followed by a particular preposition. Here are some examples of:

- nouns followed by 'to'

alternative	answer	approach	attitude
introduction	invitation	reaction	
reference	resistance	return	

> *This was my first real <u>introduction to</u> Africa.*

- nouns followed by 'for'

admiration	desire	dislike	need
reason	respect	responsibility	search
substitute	taste	thirst	

Their <u>need for</u> money is growing fast.

- nouns followed by 'on'

agreement	attack	comment	effect	tax

She had a dreadful <u>effect on</u> me.

- nouns followed by 'with' or 'between'

connection	contact	link	relationship

His illness had some <u>connection with</u> his diet.

- nouns followed by 'in'

decrease	difficulty	fall	increase	rise

They demanded a large <u>increase in</u> wages.

Unit 57: Verb + preposition

Main points

- Some verbs do not take an object and are normally followed by a preposition.
- Some verbs take an object followed by a particular preposition.
- Some verbs can take either an object or a preposition.

1 Many verbs that are used without an object are normally followed by a prepositional phrase. Some verbs take a particular preposition:

belong to	consist of	hint at	hope for
insist on	laugh at	lead to	listen to
pay for	qualify for	refer to	relate to
sympathize with			

The land <u>belongs to</u> a rich family.
She then <u>referred to</u> the Minister's report.
I find it hard to <u>sympathize with</u> her.

2 With other verbs that are used without an object, the choice of a different preposition may alter the meaning of the clause.

agree on/with	appeal for/to
apologize for/to	conform to/with
result from/in	suffer from/with

They <u>agreed on</u> a plan of action.
You <u>agreed with</u> me that we should buy a car.
His failure <u>resulted from</u> lack of attention to details.
The match <u>resulted in</u> a draw.

3 With verbs that are used without an object, different prepositions are used to introduce different types of information.

● 'about' indicates the subject matter

care	complain	dream	explain	hear
know	speak	talk	think	write

We will always <u>care about</u> freedom.
Tonight I'm going to <u>talk about</u> engines.

● 'at' indicates direction

glance	glare	grin	look	shout
smile	stare			

He <u>glanced briefly at</u> the photo.
'Hey!' she <u>shouted at</u> him.

● 'for' indicates purpose or reason

apologize	apply	ask	look	wait

He wanted to <u>apologize for</u> being late.
I'm going to <u>wait for</u> the next bus.

- 'into' indicates the object involved in a collision

bump	crash	drive	run

His car <u>crashed into</u> the wall.
She <u>drove into</u> the back of a lorry.

- 'of' indicates facts or information

hear	know	speak	talk	think

I've <u>heard of</u> him but I don't know who he is.
Do you <u>know of</u> the new plans for the sports centre?

- 'on' indicates confidence or certainty

count	depend	plan	rely

You can <u>count on</u> me.
You can <u>rely on</u> him to be polite.

- 'to' indicates the listener or reader

complain	explain	listen	say	speak
talk	write			

They <u>complained to</u> me about the noise.
Mary turned her head to <u>speak to</u> him.

- 'with' indicates someone whose opinion is the same or different

agree	argue	disagree	side

Do you <u>agree with</u> me about this?
The daughters <u>sided with</u> their mothers.

---

4 Some verbs have an object, but are also followed by a preposition.

The police <u>accused</u> him <u>of</u> murder.
They <u>borrowed</u> some money <u>from</u> the bank.

Some verbs can take either an object or a prepositional phrase with no change in meaning.

He had to fight <u>them</u>.
He was fighting <u>against history</u>.

Unit 58: Verbs and objects

Main points

- Intransitive verbs do not have an object.
- Transitive verbs have an object.
- Some verbs can be used with or without an object, depending on the situation or their meaning.

1 Many verbs do not normally have an object. They are called 'intransitive' verbs. They often refer to:

existence:	appear die disappear happen live remain
the human body:	ache bleed blush faint shiver smile
human noises:	cough cry laugh scream snore speak yawn
light, smell, vibration:	glow shine sparkle stink throb vibrate
position, movement:	arrive come depart fall flow go kneel run sit sleep stand swim wait walk work

An awful thing <u>has happened</u>.

The girl <u>screamed</u>.
I <u>waited</u>.

Note that intransitive verbs cannot be used in the passive.

---

2 Many verbs normally have an object. These verbs are called 'transitive' verbs. They are often connected with:

physical objects:	build buy carry catch cover cut destroy hit own remove sell use waste wear
senses:	feel hear see smell taste touch
feelings:	admire enjoy fear frighten hate like love need prefer surprise trust want
facts, ideas:	accept believe correct discuss expect express forget include know mean remember report
people:	address blame comfort contact convince defy kill persuade please tease thank warn

He <u>hit the ball</u> really hard.
Did you <u>see the rainbow</u>?
They both <u>enjoyed the film</u>.
She <u>reported the accident</u> to the police.

Don't <u>blame me</u>.

Note that transitive verbs can be used in the passive.

They <u>were blamed</u> for everything.

⚠ BE CAREFUL

'Have' is a transitive verb, but cannot be used in the passive. You can say 'I have a car' but not 'A car is had by me'.

3 Often, the people you are talking to know what the object is because of the situation, or because it has already been mentioned. In this case you can omit the object, even though the verb is transitive.

accept	answer	change	choose
clean	cook	draw	drive
eat	explain	forget	help
iron	know	learn	leave
paint	park	phone	read
remember	ride	sing	steal
study	type	understand	wash
watch	write		

I don't own a car. I can't <u>drive</u>.
I'll <u>cook</u> if you do the dishes.
I asked a question and George <u>answered</u>.
Both dresses are beautiful. It's difficult to <u>choose</u>.

4 Many verbs have more than one meaning, and are transitive in one meaning and intransitive in another meaning. For example, the verb 'run' is intransitive when you use it to mean 'move quickly' but transitive when you use it to mean 'manage or operate'.

call	fit	lose	manage	miss
move	play	run	show	spread

> The hare <u>runs</u> at enormous speed.
> She <u>runs a hotel</u>.
> She <u>moved</u> gracefully.
> The whole incident <u>had moved her</u> profoundly.

5 A few verbs are normally intransitive, but can be used with an object that is closely related to the verb.

dance (a dance)	die (a death)
dream (a dream)	laugh (a laugh)
live (a life)	sigh (a sigh)
smile (a smile)	

> Steve <u>smiled his thin, cruel smile</u>.
> He appears to have <u>lived the life of any other rich gentleman</u>.

Unit 59: Verbs with two objects

Main points

- Some verbs have two objects, a direct object and an indirect object.
- The indirect object can be used without a preposition, or after 'to' or 'for'.

1 Some verbs have two objects after them, a direct object and an indirect object. For example, in the sentence 'I gave John the book', 'the book' is the direct object. 'John' is the indirect object. Verbs that have two objects are sometimes called 'ditransitive' verbs.

> His uncle had <u>given</u> him books on India.
> She <u>sends</u> you her love.
> I <u>passed</u> him the cup.

2 When the indirect object is a pronoun, or another short noun phrase such as a noun with 'the', you put the indirect object in front of the direct object.

> Dad gave <u>me</u> a car.
> You promised <u>the lad</u> a job.
> He had lent <u>my cousin</u> the money.
> She bought <u>Dave and me</u> an ice cream.

3 You can also use the prepositions 'to' and 'for' to introduce the indirect object. If you do this, you put the preposition and indirect object after the direct object.

> *Jonathon handed his room key <u>to the receptionist</u>.*
> *Bill saved the last piece of chocolate cake <u>for the children</u>.*

When the indirect object consists of several words, you normally use a preposition to introduce it.

> *She taught physics and chemistry <u>to pupils at the local school</u>.*
> *I made that lamp <u>for a seventy-year-old woman</u>.*

You often use a preposition when you want to emphasize the indirect object.

> *Did you really buy that <u>for me</u>?*
> *Give the book <u>to me</u>!*

---

4 With some verbs you can only use 'for', not 'to', to introduce the indirect object.

book	buy	cook	cut
find	keep	make	paint
pour	prepare	save	win

> *They booked a place <u>for me</u>.*

The organization helps find jobs <u>for unemployed people</u>.
The two children bought a present <u>for their teacher</u>.
She sat down and painted a picture <u>for her father</u>.

5 With some verbs you normally use 'to' to introduce the indirect object.

give	lend	offer	pass	pay
post	promise	read	sell	
send	show	teach	tell	

I had lent my bicycle <u>to a friend</u>.
Ralph passed a message <u>to Jack</u>.
After tea she would read a story <u>to the children</u>.
He immediately offered his resignation <u>to the Prime Minister</u>.
They told me they posted the letter <u>to me</u> last week.
He sold it <u>to me</u>.

Note that you can use 'for' with these verbs, but it has a different meaning. 'For' indicates that one person does something on behalf of another person, so that the other person does not have to do it.

His mother paid the bill <u>for him</u>.
If you're going out, can you post this <u>for me</u>, please?

*I've forgotten my glasses. Could you read
that <u>for me</u>?*

Unit 60: Reflexive verbs

Main points

- Transitive verbs are used with a reflexive pronoun to indicate that the object is the same as the subject, for example: 'I hurt myself'.
- Some verbs which do not normally have a person as the object can have reflexive pronouns as the object.

---

1 You use a reflexive pronoun after a transitive verb to indicate that the object is the same as the subject.

> He blamed <u>himself</u> for his friend's death.
> I taught <u>myself</u> French.
> His comrades asked him if he had hurt <u>himself</u>.

→ See Unit 24 for more information on reflexive pronouns.

---

2 In theory, most transitive verbs can be used with a reflexive pronoun. However, you often use reflexive pronouns with the following verbs.

amuse	blame	cut	dry	help
hurt	introduce	kill	prepare	
repeat	restrict	satisfy	teach	

Sam <u>amused himself</u> by throwing branches into the fire.
'Please can I borrow a pencil?' – 'Yes, <u>help yourself</u>.'
<u>Prepare yourself</u> for a shock.
He <u>introduced himself</u> to me.

3 Verbs like 'dress', 'shave', and 'wash', which describe actions that people do to themselves, do not usually take reflexive pronouns in English, although they do in some other languages. With these verbs, reflexive pronouns are only used for emphasis.

I <u>dressed</u> in a hurry and left.
She had <u>dressed herself</u> entirely in white.
I usually <u>shave</u> before breakfast.
He prefers to <u>shave himself</u>, even with that broken arm.
She <u>washed</u> very quickly and rushed downstairs.
The children were encouraged to <u>wash themselves</u>.

4 'Behave' does not normally take an object at all, but can take a reflexive pronoun as the object.

> If they don't <u>behave</u>, send them straight up to bed.
>
> He is old enough to know how to <u>behave himself</u>.

5 Some verbs do not normally have a person as the object, because they describe actions that you do not do to other people. However, these verbs can have reflexive pronouns as the object, because you can do these actions to yourself.

apply	compose	distance	enjoy
excel	exert	express	strain

> I really <u>enjoyed</u> the party.
>
> Just go out there, have a good time, and <u>enjoy yourself</u>.
>
> She <u>expressed</u> surprise at the news that he had returned.
>
> Professor Dale <u>expressed himself</u> very forcibly indeed.

6 When 'busy' and 'content' are used as verbs, they always take a reflexive pronoun as their direct object. They are therefore true 'reflexive verbs'.

He had <u>busied himself</u> in the laboratory.
I had to <u>content myself</u> with watching the
little moving lights.

Unit 61: Reciprocal verbs

Main points

- Some verbs describe two people or two groups of people doing the same thing to each other, for example: 'We met', 'I met you', 'We met each other'.

- You use 'each other' or 'one another' for emphasis. There is no difference in meaning between 'each other' and 'one another'.

- With some verbs, you use 'each other' or 'one another' after 'with'.

1 Some verbs refer to actions that involve two people or two groups of people doing the same thing to each other. These verbs are sometimes called 'reciprocal' verbs.

> _We met_ in Delhi.
> _Jane and Sarah told me that <u>they met you</u>._
> _<u>They met each other</u>_ for the very first time last week.

2 The two people or groups of people involved in the action are often mentioned as the plural subject of the verb, and the verb does not have an object.

For example, 'John and Mary argued' means that John argued with Mary and Mary argued with John.

argue	clash	coincide	combine
compete	fight	kiss	marry
match	meet		

The pair of you <u>have argued</u> about that for years.
We <u>competed</u> furiously.
Their children <u>are always fighting</u>.
They <u>kissed</u>.

---

3 When you want to emphasize that both people or groups of people are equally involved, you can use the pronouns 'each other' or 'one another' as the object of the verb. Verbs that refer to actions in which there is physical contact between people are often used with 'each other' or 'one another'.

| cuddle | embrace | fight | hug | kiss | touch |

We embraced <u>each other</u>.
They fought <u>one another</u> desperately for it.
They kissed <u>each other</u> in greeting.
It was the first time they had touched <u>one another</u>.

Note that there is no difference in meaning between 'each other' and 'one another'.

---

4 Some verbs do not take an object, so you use a preposition before 'each other' or 'one another'.

> They _parted from each other_ after only two weeks.
> We _talk to one another_ as often as possible.

---

5 With some verbs you have a choice of preposition before 'each other' or 'one another'. For example, you can 'fight with' one another or 'fight against' one another.

with/against:	compete fight
with/from:	part
with/to:	correspond relate talk

> Many countries are _competing with each other_.
> Did you _compete against each other_ in yesterday's race?
> Stephen and I _parted with one another_ on good terms.
> They _parted from one another_ quite suddenly.

6 With some verbs, you can only use 'with' before 'each other' or 'one another'.

Note that most of these verbs refer to people talking or working together.

agree	argue	clash
collide	communicate	co-operate
disagree	quarrel	

We do <u>agree with each other</u> sometimes.
Have they <u>communicated with each other</u> since then?
The two lorries <u>collided with one another</u> on the motorway.

7 If you want to focus on one of the people involved, you make them the subject of the verb and make the other person the object.

<u>She</u> married <u>a young engineer</u>.
<u>You</u> could meet <u>me</u> at the restaurant.

If the verb cannot take an object, you mention the other person after a preposition.

Youths clashed <u>with police</u> in Belfast.
She was always quarrelling <u>with him</u>.

Unit 62: Linking verbs

Main points

- Linking verbs are used to join the subject with a complement.
- Linking verbs can have adjectives, noun phrases, or 'to'-infinitive clauses as complements.
- You can use 'it' and 'there' as impersonal subjects with linking verbs.

1 A small but important group of verbs are followed by a complement rather than an object. The complement tells you more about the subject. Verbs that take complements are called 'linking' verbs.

appear	be	become	feel	get
go	grow	keep	look	
prove	remain	seem	smell	
sound	stay	taste	turn	

> I _am_ proud of these people.
> She _was getting_ too old to play tennis.
> They _looked_ all right to me.

2 Linking verbs often have adjectives as complements describing the subject.

We <u>felt</u> very happy.
He <u>was</u> the tallest in the room.
You <u>seem</u> surprised.

---

3 You can use linking verbs with noun phrases as complements to give your opinion about the subject.

He's not <u>the right man for the job</u>.
She seemed <u>an ideal person to look after them</u>.

You also use noun phrases as complements after 'be', 'become', and 'remain' to specify the subject.

He became <u>a geologist</u>.
Promises by MPs remained just <u>promises</u>.
This one is <u>yours</u>.

Note that you use object pronouns after 'be'.

It's <u>me</u> again.
That's <u>her</u> in the blue dress.

---

4 Some linking verbs can have 'to'-infinitive clauses as complements.

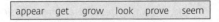

| appear | get | grow | look | prove | seem |

He appears <u>to have taken my keys</u>.
She seemed <u>to like me</u>.

241

These verbs, and 'remain', can also be followed by 'to be' and a complement.

> Mary <u>seemed to be</u> asleep.
> His new job <u>proved to be</u> a challenge.
> A number of serious problems <u>remained to be</u> settled.

5 You can use 'it' and 'there' as impersonal subjects with linking verbs.

> It <u>seems</u> silly not to tell him.
> It <u>became</u> clear that she was ill.
> There <u>appears</u> to have been a terrible mistake.

→ See Units 21 and 22 for more information.

You can use 'be' with some abstract nouns as the subject, followed by a 'that'-clause or a 'to'-infinitive clause as the complement.

advice	agreement	answer	decision
idea	plan	problem	solution

> <u>The answer is</u> that they are simply not interested in it.
> <u>The idea was</u> to spend more money on basic training.

Some can only have a 'that'-clause.

conclusion	explanation	fact
feeling	reason	report
thought	understanding	

The fact is that I can't go to the party.

Unit 63: Phrasal verbs

Main points

- A phrasal verb is a combination of a verb and an adverb or preposition.
- The usual meaning of the verb is normally altered.
- Phrasal verbs are used in four main structures.

1 Phrasal verbs are verbs that combine with adverbs or prepositions. The adverbs and prepositions are called particles, for example 'down', 'in', 'off', 'out', and 'up'.

> She _turned off_ the radio.
> Mr Knight offered to _put_ him _up_.

2 Phrasal verbs extend the usual meaning of the verb or create a new meaning. For example, if you 'break' something, you damage it, but if you 'break out of' a place, you escape from it.

> They _broke out of_ prison on Thursday night.
> The pain gradually _wore off_.

3 Phrasal verbs are normally used in one of four main structures. In the first structure,

the verb is followed by a particle, and
there is no object.

break out	catch on	check up	come in
get by	give in	go away	grow up
look in	ring off	start out	stay up
stop off	wait up	watch out	wear off

War <u>broke out</u> in September.
You'll have to <u>stay up</u> late tonight.

---

4 In the second structure, the verb is
followed by a particle and an object.

fall for	feel for	grow on	look after
part with	pick on	take after	

She <u>looked after her invalid mother</u>.
This music is beginning to <u>grow on me</u>.

---

5 In the third structure, the verb is followed
by an object and a particle.

answer back	ask in	call back
catch out	count in	invite out
order about	tell apart	

I <u>answered him back</u> and took my chances.
He loved to <u>order people about</u>.

6 Many phrasal verbs can be used in both the second structure and the third structure: verb followed by a particle and an object, or verb followed by an object and a particle.

add on	bring up	call up
clean up	hand over	knock over
point out	pull down	put away
put up	rub out	sort out
take up	tear up	throw away
try out		

> *It took ages for Josephine to <u>clean up the mess</u>.*
> *It took ages for Josephine to <u>clean the mess up</u>.*
> *There was such a mess. It took ages for Josephine to <u>clean it up</u>.*

⚠ BE CAREFUL

In these cases, if the object is a pronoun, it must go in front of the particle. You cannot say 'He cleaned up it'.

7 In the fourth structure, the verb is followed by a particle and a preposition with an object.

break out of	catch up with
come down with	get on with
go down with	keep on at
look forward to	make off with
miss out on	play around with
put up with	run away with
stick up for	talk down to
walk out on	

You go on ahead. I'll <u>catch up with you</u> later.
Children have to learn to <u>stick up for themselves</u>.

8 A very few verbs are used in the structure: verb followed by an object, a particle, and a preposition with its object.

do out of	let in for	put down to
put up to	take out on	take up on
talk out of		

I'll <u>take you up on that generous invitation</u>.
Joe tried to <u>talk her out of it</u>.

Unit 64: Common verb + noun patterns

Main points

- Examples are: 'have a bath'; 'give a shout'; 'make promises'; 'take care'.
- Common verbs are often used with nouns to describe actions.
- You use 'have' with nouns referring to eating, drinking, talking, and washing.
- You use 'give' with nouns referring to noises, hitting, and talking.
- You use 'make' with nouns referring to talking, plans, and travelling.

1 When you want to talk about actions, you often use common verbs with nouns as their object. The nouns describe the action. For example, if you say 'I had a shower', the noun tells you what the action was. The common verbs have very little meaning.

> I *had a nice rest*.
> She *made a remark* about the weather.

The nouns often have related verbs that do not take an object.

248

Common verb + noun patterns   Unit 64

Helen went upstairs to <u>rest</u>.
I <u>remarked</u> that it would be better if I came.

2 Different verbs are used with different nouns. You use 'have' with nouns referring to:

meals:	breakfast dinner drink lunch meal taste tea
talking:	chat conversation discussion talk
washing:	bath shower wash
relaxation:	break holiday rest
disagreement:	argument fight quarrel trouble

We usually <u>have lunch</u> at one o'clock.
He was <u>having his first holiday</u> for five years.

3 You use 'give' with nouns referring to:

human noises:	cry gasp giggle groan laugh scream shout sigh whistle yell
facial expressions:	grin smile
hitting:	kick punch push slap
talking:	advice answer example information interview lecture news report speech talk warning

> Mr Sutton _gave a shout_ of triumph.
> She _gave a long lecture_ about Roosevelt.

4 You use 'make' with nouns referring to:

talking and sounds:	comment enquiry
	noise point promise
	remark sound speech
	suggestion
plans:	arrangement choice
	decision plan
travelling:	journey tour trip visit

> He _made the shortest speech_ I've ever heard.
> In 1978 he _made his first visit_ to Australia.

5 You use 'take' with these nouns:

care	chance	charge
decision	interest	offence
photograph	responsibility	risk
time	trouble .	turns

> He was _taking no chances_.
> She was prepared to _take great risks_.

6 You use 'go' and 'come' with '-ing' nouns referring to sports and outdoor activities.

> She _goes climbing_ in her holidays.
> Every morning, he _goes jogging_ with Tommy.

Note that you can also use 'go for' and 'come for' with 'a jog', 'a run', 'a swim', 'a walk'.

> *They <u>went for a run</u> before breakfast.*
> *Would you like to <u>come for a walk</u> with me?*

---

7 You use 'do' with '-ing' nouns referring to jobs connected with the home, and nouns referring generally to work.

> *He wants to <u>do the cooking</u>.*
> *He <u>does all the shopping</u> and I <u>do the washing</u>.*
> *The man who <u>did the job</u> had ten years' training.*
> *He has to get up early and <u>do a hard day's work</u>.*

'Do' is often used instead of more specific verbs. For example, you can say 'Have you done your teeth?' instead of 'Have you brushed your teeth?'

> *Do I need to <u>do my hair</u>?*

Unit 65: Auxiliary verbs

Main points

- The auxiliaries 'be', 'have', and 'do' are used to make verb forms, negatives, and questions.

- The auxiliary 'be' is used in forming the progressive and the passive.

- The auxiliary 'have' is used in forming the perfect.

- The auxiliary 'do' is used in making negative and question forms from sentences that have a verb in a simple form.

1 The auxiliary verbs are 'be', 'have', and 'do'. They are used with a main verb to make verb forms, negatives, and questions.

He _is_ planning to get married soon.
I _haven't_ seen Peter since last night.
Which doctor _do_ you want to see?

2 'Be' as an auxiliary is used:

- with the '-ing' form of the main verb to form the progressive

He _is_ living in Germany.
They _were_ going to phone you.

- with the '-ed' participle of the main verb
  to form the passive

  These cars <u>are</u> made in Japan.
  *The walls of her flat <u>were</u> covered with
  posters.*

---

3 You use 'have' as an auxiliary with the '-ed'
participle to form the perfect.

  I <u>have</u> changed my mind.
  I wish you <u>had</u> met Guy.

The present perfect progressive, the past
perfect progressive, and perfect forms in
the passive, are formed using both 'have'
and 'be'.

  He <u>has been</u> working very hard recently.
  *She did not know how long she <u>had been</u>
  lying there.*
  The guest-room window <u>has been</u> mended.
  They <u>had been</u> taught by a young teacher.

---

4 'Be' and 'have' are also used as auxiliaries in
negative sentences and questions in
progressive and perfect forms, and in the
passive.

  He <u>isn't</u> going.
  <u>Hasn't</u> she seen it yet?
  <u>Was</u> it written in English?

You use 'do' as an auxiliary to make

negative and question forms from
sentences that have a verb in the present
simple or past simple.

> He _doesn't_ think he can come to the party.
> _Do_ you like her new haircut?
> She _didn't_ buy the house.
> _Didn't_ he get the job?

Note that you can use 'do' as a main verb
with the auxiliary 'do'.

> He _didn't do_ his homework.
> _Do_ they _do_ the work themselves?

You can also use the auxiliary 'do' with
'have' as a main verb.

> He _doesn't have_ any money.
> _Does_ anyone _have_ a question?

You only use 'do' in affirmative sentences
for emphasis or contrast.

> I _do_ feel sorry for Roger.

⚠ BE CAREFUL

You never use the auxiliary 'do' with 'be'
except in the imperative.

> _Don't be_ stupid!
> _Do be_ a good boy and sit still.

---

5 Some grammars include modals among
   the auxiliary verbs. When there is a modal
   in the verb phrase, it is always the first

word in the verb phrase, and comes
before the auxiliaries 'be' and 'have'.

> *She <u>might be</u> going to Switzerland for*
> *Christmas.*
> *I <u>would have</u> liked to have seen her.*

Note that you never use the auxiliary 'do'
with a modal.

Unit 66: Present tense forms

Main points

- There are four forms of the present tense – present simple ('I walk'), present progressive ('I am walking'), present perfect ('I have walked'), and present perfect progressive ('I have been walking').

- All these forms are used to refer to a time which includes the present.

- These forms can also be used for predictions made in the present about future events.

1 There are four verb forms which begin with a verb in the present tense. They are the present simple, the present progressive, the present perfect, and the present perfect progressive.

The present simple form of a verb is the same as the base form, except in the third person singular, where 's' is added to the base form.

> I <u>walk</u> to work every day.
> Susan <u>walks</u> to work every day.

The present progressive is formed by using

the present tense of 'be' and the '-ing' participle of the main verb.

He is walking home.

The present perfect is formed by using the present tense of 'have' and the '-ed' participle of the main verb.

I have walked five miles already.

The present perfect progressive is formed by using the present perfect of 'be' and the '-ing' participle of the main verb.

She has been walking for hours.

---

2 The present simple and the present progressive are used with reference to present time. If you are talking about the general present, or about a regular or habitual action, you use the present simple.

George lives in Birmingham.
They often phone my mother in London.

If you are talking about something in the present situation, you use the present progressive.

He's playing tennis at the University.
I'm cooking the dinner.

The present progressive is often used to refer to a temporary situation.

She's living in a flat at the moment.

3 You use the present perfect or the present perfect progressive when you are concerned with the present effects of something which happened at a time in the past, or which started in the past but is still continuing.

> *Have* you *seen* this film yet?
> We*'ve been waiting* here since before two o'clock.

4 If you are talking about something which is scheduled or timetabled to happen in the future, you can use the present simple.

> The next train *leaves* at two fifteen in the morning.
> It*'s* Tuesday tomorrow.

5 If you are talking about something which has been arranged for the future, you can use the present progressive. When you use the present progressive like this, there is nearly always a time adverbial like 'tomorrow', 'next week', or 'later' in the clause.

> We*'re going* on holiday with my parents this year.
> The Browns *are having* a birthday party next week.
> Later on I*'m speaking* to Patty.

6 It is only in the main clauses that the choice of verb form can be related to a particular time. In subordinate clauses, for example in 'if'-clauses, time clauses, and defining relative clauses, present forms often refer to a future time in relation to the time in the main clause.

> You can go at eleven thirty _if_ you _have finished_.
> Let's have something to eat and drink _before_ we _start_.
> We'll save some food for anyone _who arrives_ late.

7 The present simple normally has no auxiliary verb, but questions and negative sentences are formed with the auxiliary 'do'.

> _Do_ you _live_ round here?
> _Does_ your husband _do_ most of the cooking?
> They _don't_ often _phone_ during the week.
> She _doesn't like_ being late if she can help it.

Unit 67: Past tense forms

Main points

- There are four forms of the past tense – past simple ('I walked'), past progressive ('I was walking'), past perfect ('I had walked'), and past perfect progressive ('I had been walking').

- All these forms are used to refer to past time.

- They are often used as polite forms.

- They have special meanings in conditional clauses and when referring to imaginary situations.

1 There are four verb forms which begin with a verb in the past tense. They are the past simple, the past progressive, the past perfect, and the past perfect progressive. They are used to refer to past time, and also to refer to imaginary situations, and to express politeness.

The past simple of a regular verb is formed by adding 'ed' to the base form of the regular verb.

   I <u>walked</u> home.

There are also many verbs with irregular

past tense forms.

See pages 474–479 for a list of irregular past tense forms.

The past progressive is formed by using the past tense of 'be' and the '-ing' participle of the main verb.

He <u>was walking</u> home when he saw her.

The past perfect is formed by using 'had' and the '-ed' participle of the main verb.

She <u>had walked</u> for miles that day.

The past perfect progressive is formed by using 'had been' and the '-ing' participle of the main verb.

I <u>had been walking</u> all morning.

---

2 The past simple and the past progressive are used with reference to past time. You use the past simple for events which happened in the past.

I <u>woke up</u> early and <u>got</u> out of bed.
I <u>caught</u> my dress on the fence.

If you are talking about the general past, or about regular or habitual actions in the past, you also use the past simple.

She <u>lived</u> just outside London.
We often <u>saw</u> his dog sitting outside his house.

If you are talking about something which continued to happen before and after a particular time in the past, you use the past progressive.

They <u>were sitting</u> in the kitchen, when they heard the explosion.
Jack arrived while the children <u>were having</u> their bath.

The past progressive is often used to refer to a temporary situation.

He <u>was working</u> at home at the time.
Bill <u>was using</u> my office until I came back from America.

3 You use the past perfect and past perfect progressive when you are talking about the past and you are concerned with something which happened at an earlier time, or which had started at an earlier time but was still continuing.

I <u>had heard</u> it was a good film so we decided to go and see it.
It was getting late. I <u>had been waiting</u> there since two o'clock.

4 You sometimes use a past tense form rather than a present tense form when you want to be more polite. For example, in the following pairs of sentences, the

second one is more polite.

> <u>Do</u> you <u>want</u> to see me now?
> <u>Did</u> you <u>want</u> to see me now?
> I <u>wonder</u> if you can help me.
> I <u>was wondering</u> if you could help me.

5 The past tense forms have special
   meanings in conditional clauses and when
   referring to hypothetical and imaginary
   situations, for example after 'I wish' or
   'What if...?'. You use the past simple and
   past progressive for something that you
   think is unlikely to happen.

> If they <u>saw</u> the mess, they would be
> extremely angry.
> We would certainly tell you if we <u>were selling</u>
> the house.
> What if you <u>asked</u> her for the money instead?

You use the past perfect and past perfect
progressive when you are talking about
something which could have happened in
the past, but which did not actually
happen.

> If I <u>had known</u> that you were coming,
> I would have told Jim.
> They wouldn't have gone to bed if they
> <u>had been expecting</u> you to arrive.

Unit 68: The progressive

Main points

- The progressive is made of a form of 'be' and an '-ing' participle.

- The progressive describes actions which continue to happen before and after a particular time.

- The progressive can also indicate duration and change.

1 The progressive is made of a form of 'be' and an '-ing' participle.

You use the progressive to indicate that an action continues to happen before and after a particular time, without stopping. You use the present progressive for actions which continue to happen before and after the moment of speaking.

> I'_m looking_ at the photos my brother sent me.
> They'_re having_ a meeting.

2 When you are talking about two actions in the present tense, you use the present progressive for an action that continues to happen before and after another action that interrupts it. You use the present simple for the other action.

> *The phone always rings when I'm having a bath.*
> *Friends always talk to me when I'm trying to study.*

3 When you are talking about the past, you use the past progressive for actions that continued to happen before and after another action, or before and after a particular time. This is often called the 'interrupted past'. You use the past simple for the other action.

> *He was watching television when the doorbell rang.*
> *It was 6 o'clock. The train was nearing London.*

⚠ **BE CAREFUL**

If two things happened one after another, you use two verbs in the past simple.

> *As soon as he saw me, he waved.*

4 You can use progressive forms with modals in all their usual meanings.

> *What could he be thinking of?*
> *They might be telling lies.*

5 You use the progressive to express duration, when you want to emphasize the length of a situation.

> We _had been living_ in Athens for five years.
> They'_ll be staying_ with us for a couple of weeks.
> He _has been building up_ the business all his life.
> By 1992, he _will have been working_ for ten years.

Note that you do not have to use the progressive for duration.

> We _had lived_ in Africa for five years.
> He _worked_ for us for ten years.

6 You use the progressive to describe a state or situation that is temporary.

> I'_m living_ in London at the moment.
> He'_ll be working_ nights next week.
> She'_s spending_ the summer in Europe.

7 You use the progressive to show that something is changing, developing, or progressing.

> Her English _was improving_.
> The children _are growing up_ quickly.
> The video industry _has been developing_ rapidly.

8 As a general rule, verbs which refer to actions that require a deliberate effort can be used in the progressive, while verbs which refer to actions that do not require a deliberate effort are not usually used in the progressive.

> I _think_ it's going to rain. ('think'= 'believe'. Believing does not require deliberate effort)
> Please be quiet. I'_m thinking_. ('think'= 'try to solve a problem'. Trying to solve a problem does require deliberate effort)

However, many verbs are not normally used in the progressive. These include verbs that refer to thinking, liking and disliking, appearance, possession, and perception.

→ See Unit 70 for lists of these verbs.

Unit 69: The perfect

Main points

- The perfect is made of a form of 'have' and an '-ed' participle.
- You use the present perfect ('I have walked') to relate the past to the present.
- You use the past perfect ('I had walked') to talk about a situation that occurred before a particular time in the past.

1 The perfect is made of a form of 'have' and an '-ed' participle.

You use the present perfect when you are concerned with the present effects of something which happened at an indefinite time in the past.

I'm afraid I've forgotten my book.
Have you heard from Jill recently?

Sometimes, the present effects are important because they are very recent.

Karen has just passed her exams.

You also use the present perfect when you are thinking of a time which started in the past and is still continuing.

Have you really lived here for ten years?
He has worked here since 1987.

You also use the present perfect in time clauses, when you are talking about something which will be done at some time in the future.

Tell me when you have finished.
I'll write to you as soon as I have heard from Jenny.

---

2 When you want to emphasize the fact that a recent event continued to happen for some time, you use the present perfect progressive.

She's been crying.
I've been working hard all day.

---

3 You use the past perfect when you are looking back from a point in past time, and you are concerned with the effects of something which happened at an earlier time in the past.

I apologized because I had forgotten my book again.
He felt much happier once he had found a new job.
Mr and Mrs Jones would have come if we had invited them.

269

You also use the past perfect when you are thinking of a time which had started earlier in the past but was still continuing.

> *I was about twenty. I <u>had been studying</u> French for a couple of years.*
> *He hated games and <u>had always managed</u> to avoid children's parties.*

---

4 You use the future perfect when you are looking back from a point in the future and you are talking about something which will have happened at a time between now and that future point.

> *In another two years, you <u>will have left</u> school.*
> *Take these tablets, and in twenty-four hours the pain <u>will have gone</u>.*

You also use the future perfect when you are looking back from the present and guessing that an action will be finished.

> *I'm sure they <u>will have arrived</u> at the airport by now.*
> *It's too late to ring Don. He <u>will have left</u> the house by now.*

---

5 You can also use other modals with 'have', when you are looking back from a point in time at something which you think may have happened at an earlier time.

I *might have finished* work by then.
He *should have arrived* in Paris by the time
we phone.

For more information on modals with
'have',

→ See Units 87 to 99.

Unit 70: Talking about the present

Main points

- For the general present, general truths, and habitual actions, you use the present simple ('I walk').

- For something which is happening now, or for temporary situations, you use the present progressive ('I am walking').

1 If you are talking about the present in general, you normally use the present simple. You use the present simple for talking about the general present including the present moment.

> *My dad <u>works</u> in Saudi Arabia.*
> *He <u>lives</u> in the French Alps near the Swiss border.*

2 If you are talking about general truths, you use the present simple.

> *Water <u>boils</u> at 100 degrees centigrade.*
> *Love <u>makes</u> the world go round.*
> *The bus <u>takes</u> longer than the train.*

3 If you are talking about regular or habitual actions, you use the present simple.

> <u>Do</u> you <u>eat</u> meat?
> I <u>get</u> up early and <u>eat</u> my breakfast in bed.
> I usually <u>finish</u> work early on Fridays.

4 If you are talking about something which is regarded as temporary, you use the present progressive.

> Do you know if she'<u>s</u> still <u>playing</u> tennis these days?
> I'<u>m working</u> as a British Council officer.
> She <u>is studying</u> French at the University of East Anglia.

5 If you are talking about something which is happening now, you normally use the present progressive.

> We'<u>re having</u> a meeting. Come and join in.
> Wait a moment. I'<u>m listening</u> to the news.

6 There are a number of verbs which are used in the present simple even when you are talking about the present moment. These verbs are not normally used in the present or past progressive.

These verbs usually refer to:

thinking:	believe forget imagine know realize recognize suppose think understand want wish
liking and disliking:	admire dislike hate like love prefer
appearance:	appear look like resemble seem
possession:	belong to contain have include own possess
perception:	hear see smell taste
being:	be consist of exist

I believe he was not to blame.
She hates going to parties.
Our neighbours have two cars.

Note that you normally use verbs of perception with the modal 'can', rather than using the present simple.

I can smell gas.

Note that some of these verbs can be used in perfect progressive forms.

I have been wanting to see that film for ages.
John had been keeping birds for years.

Some of these verbs, especially 'love' and 'like', can be used in the present or past progressive in very informal English.

I'm loving your new hairstyle!

Some other common verbs are not normally used in the present progressive or the other progressive forms.

concern	deserve	fit	interest	involve
matter	mean	satisfy	surprise	

What do you mean?

⚠️ **BE CAREFUL**

Some of the verbs listed above can be used in the progressive in other meanings. For example, 'have' referring to possession is not used in the progressive. You do not say 'I am having a car'. But note the following examples.

We're having a party tomorrow.
He's having problems with his car.
She's having a shower.

Unit 71: Talking about the past

Main points

- For actions, situations, or regular events in the past, you use the past simple ('I walked'). For regular events in the past, you can also use 'would' or 'used to'.

- For events that happened before and after a time in the past, and for temporary situations, you use the past progressive ('I was walking').

- For present effects of past situations, you use the present perfect ('I have walked'), and for past effects of earlier events you use the past perfect ('I had walked').

- For future in the past, you use 'would', 'was/were going to', or the past progressive ('I was walking').

1 When you want to talk about an event that occurred at a particular time in the past, you use the past simple.

> The Prime Minister _flew_ into New York yesterday.
> The new term _started_ last week.

You also use the past simple to talk about a situation that existed over a period of time in the past.

We <u>spent</u> most of our time at home last winter.
They <u>earned</u> their money quickly that year.

2 When you want to talk about something which took place regularly in the past, you use the past simple.

They <u>went</u> for picnics most weekends.
We usually <u>spent</u> the winter at Aunt Meg's house.

⚠ BE CAREFUL

The past simple always refers to a time in the past. A time reference is necessary to say what time in the past you are referring to. The time reference can be established in an earlier sentence or by another speaker, but it must be established.

When you want to talk about something which occurred regularly in the past, you can use 'would' or 'used to' instead of the past simple.

We <u>would</u> normally <u>spend</u> the winter in Miami.
People <u>used to believe</u> that the world was flat.

> ⚠ **BE CAREFUL**
>
> You do not normally use 'would' with this meaning with verbs which are not used in the progressive.
>
> → For a list of these verbs, see Unit 70.

---

3 When you want to talk about something which continued to happen before and after a given time in the past, you use the past progressive.

> *I hurt myself when I <u>was mending</u> my bike.*
> *It was midnight. She <u>was driving</u> home.*

You also use the past progressive to talk about a temporary state of affairs in the past.

> *Our team <u>were losing</u> 2-1 at the time.*
> *We <u>were staying</u> with friends in Italy.*

→ For more information on the progressive, see Unit 68.

---

4 When you are concerned with the present effects or future effects of something which happened at an indefinite time in the past, you use the present perfect.

> *I'm afraid I <u>'ve forgotten</u> my book, so I don't know.*
> *<u>Have</u> you <u>heard</u> from Jill recently? How is she?*

You also use the present perfect when you are thinking of a time which started in the past and still continues.

> _Have_ you ever _stolen_ anything? (= at any time up to the present)
> He _has been_ here since six o'clock. (= and he is still here)

5 When you are looking back from a point in past time, and you are concerned with the effects of something which happened at an earlier time in the past, you use the past perfect.

> I apologized because I _had left_ my wallet at home.
> They would have come if we _had invited_ them.

6 When you want to talk about the future from a point of view in past time, you can use 'would', 'was/were going to', or the past progressive.

> He thought to himself how wonderful it _would taste_.
> Her daughter _was going to_ do the cooking.
> Mike _was taking_ his test the week after.

Unit 72: 'Will' and 'going to'

Main points

- When you are making predictions about the future or talking about future intentions, you can use either 'will' ('I will walk') or 'going to' ('I am going to walk').

- For promises and offers relating to the future, you use 'will' ('I will walk').

- For future events based on arrangements, you use the future progressive ('I will be walking').

- For events that will happen before a time in the future, you use the future perfect ('I will have walked').

1 You cannot talk about the future with as much certainty as you can about the present or the past. You are usually talking about what you think might happen or what you intend to happen. This is why you often use modals. Although most modals can be used with future reference, you most often use the modal 'will' to talk about the future.

> Nancy _will arrange_ it.
> When _will_ I _see_ them?

2 When you are making predictions about the future that are based on general beliefs, opinions, or attitudes, you use 'will'.

The weather tomorrow <u>will be</u> warm and sunny.
I'm sure you <u>will enjoy</u> your visit to the zoo.

This use of 'will' is common in sentences with conditional clauses.

You<u>'ll be</u> late, if you don't hurry.

When you are using facts or events in the present situation as evidence for a prediction, you can use 'going to'.

It<u>'s going to rain</u>. (I can see black clouds)
I<u>'m going to be late</u>. (I have missed my train)

3 When you are talking about your own intentions, you use 'will' or 'going to'.

I<u>'ll ring you</u> tonight.
I<u>'m going to stay</u> at home today.

When you are saying what someone else has decided to do, you use 'going to'.

They<u>'re going to have</u> a party.
She<u>'s going to be</u> an actress.

⚠ BE CAREFUL

You do not normally use 'going to' with the verb 'go'. You usually just say 'I'm going' rather than 'I'm going to go'.

> *'What <u>are you going to</u> do this weekend?' –*
> *'I'<u>m going</u> to the cinema.'*

When you are announcing a decision you have just made or are about to make, you use 'will'.

> *I'm tired. I think I'<u>ll go</u> to bed.*

---

4 In promises and offers relating to the future, you often use 'will' with the meaning 'be willing to'.

> *I'<u>ll do</u> what I can.*
> *I'<u>ll help</u> with the washing-up.*

Note that you can use 'will' with this meaning in an 'if'-clause.

> *I'll put you through, if you'<u>ll hang on</u> for a minute.* (= if you are willing to hang on for a minute)

⚠ BE CAREFUL

Remember that you do not normally use 'will' in 'if'-clauses.

→ See Unit 74 for more information on 'if'-clauses.

> *If you <u>do</u> that, you will be wasting your time.*

The children will call out if they <u>think</u> he is wrong.

---

5 When you want to say that something will happen because arrangements have been made, you use the future progressive.

The future progressive is formed by using 'will' or 'shall' followed by 'be' and the '-ing' participle of the main verb.

> *I'll <u>be seeing</u> them when I've finished with you.*
> *I'll <u>be waiting</u> for you outside.*
> *She'll <u>be appearing</u> at the Royal Festival Hall.*

---

6 When you want to talk about something that has not happened yet but will happen before a particular time in the future, you use the future perfect.

The future perfect is formed by using 'will' or 'shall' followed by 'have' and the '-ed' participle of the main verb.

> *By the time we phone he'll already <u>have started</u>.*
> *By 2010, he <u>will have worked</u> for twelve years.*

Unit 73: Present forms for future

Main points

- When you are talking about the future in relation to official timetables or the calendar, you use the present simple ('I walk').

- When talking about people's plans and arrangements for the future, you use the present progressive ('I am walking').

- In 'if'-clauses, time clauses, and defining relative clauses, you can use the present simple ('I walk') to refer to the future.

1 When you are talking about something in the future which is based on an official timetable or calendar, you use the present simple. You usually put a time adverbial in these sentences.

> My train *leaves* Euston *at 11.30* on Tuesday morning.
> The UN General Assembly *opens* in New York *this month*.
> Our next lesson *is on Thursday*.
> We *set off early tomorrow morning*.

2 In statements about fixed dates, you normally use the present simple.

> Tomorrow <u>is</u> Tuesday.
> It'<u>s</u> my birthday next month.
> Monday <u>is</u> the seventeenth of July.

3 When you want to talk about people's plans or arrangements for the future, you use the present progressive.

> I'<u>m meeting</u> Bill next week.
> They'<u>re getting married</u> in June.
> We'<u>re going</u> to Barbados at the beginning of September.

4 You often talk about the future using the present tense of verbs such as 'hope', 'expect', 'intend', and 'want' with a 'to'-infinitive clause, especially when you want to indicate your uncertainty about what will actually happen.

> We <u>hope to see</u> you soon.
> Bill <u>expects to be</u> back at work tomorrow morning.
> They <u>intend to press ahead</u> with plans to scrap the current system.

After the verb 'hope', you often use the present simple to refer to the future.

> I hope you <u>enjoy</u> your holiday.

5 In subordinate clauses, the relationships between tense and time are different. In 'if'-clauses and time clauses, you normally use the present simple for future reference.

> *If he <u>comes</u>, I'll let you know.*
> *Please start when you <u>are</u> ready.*
> *We won't start the meeting until everyone <u>arrives</u>.*
> *Don't forget to lock the door after you <u>leave</u>.*

6 In defining relative clauses, you normally use the present simple, not 'will', to refer to the future.

> *Any decision <u>that you make</u> will need her approval.*
> *Give my love to any friends <u>you meet</u> at the party.*
> *There is a gold cup for the runner <u>who finishes first</u>.*
> *<u>Whoever replaces</u> her is going to have a difficult job.*

7 If you want to show that a condition has to be the case before an action can be carried out, you use the present perfect for future events.

> *We won't start until everyone <u>has arrived</u>.*

I'll let you know when I <u>have arranged</u>
everything.
She can have the toy back once <u>she has
calmed down</u>.

Unit 74: Conditionals using 'if'

Main points

- You use conditional clauses to talk about a possible situation and its results.
- Conditional clauses can begin with 'if'.
- A conditional clause needs a main clause to make a complete sentence. The conditional clause can come before or after the main clause.

1 You use conditional clauses to talk about a situation that might possibly happen and to say what its results might be.

You use 'if' to mention events and situations that happen often, that may happen in the future, that could have happened in the past but did not happen, or that are unlikely to happen at all.

> _If_ the light comes on, the battery is OK.
> I'll call you _if_ I need you.
> _If_ I had known, I'd have told you.
> _If_ she asked me, I'd help her.

2 When you are talking about something
that is generally true or happens often,
you use a present tense form in the main
clause and the conditional clause.

> If they *lose* weight during an illness, they
> soon *regain* it afterwards.
> If an advertisement *does not tell* the truth,
> the advertiser *is committing* an offence.
> If the baby *is crying*, it *is* probably hungry.
> If they *have lost* any money, they *report* it
> to me.

⚠ **BE CAREFUL**

You do not use the present progressive in
both clauses. You do not say 'If they are
losing money, they are getting angry.'

3 When you use a conditional clause with
a present tense form, you often use an
imperative in the main clause.

> *Wake* me *up* if you're worried.
> If he has finished, *ask* him to leave quietly.
> If you are very early, *don't expect* them to
> be ready.

4 When you are talking about something
which may possibly happen in the future,
you use a present tense form in the
conditional clause, and the simple future
in the main clause.

If I <u>marry</u> Celia, we <u>will need</u> the money.
If you <u>are going</u> to America, you <u>will need</u> a visa.
If he <u>has done</u> the windows, he <u>will want</u> his money.

⚠ BE CAREFUL

You do not normally use 'will' in conditional clauses. You do not say 'If I will see you tomorrow, I will give you the book'.

5 When you are talking about something that you think is unlikely to happen, you use the past simple or past progressive in the conditional clause and 'would' in the main clause.

If I <u>had</u> enough money, I <u>would buy</u> the car.
If he <u>was coming</u>, he <u>would ring</u>.

⚠ BE CAREFUL

You do not normally use 'would' in conditional clauses. You do not say 'If I would do it, I would do it like this'.

6 'Were' is sometimes used instead of 'was' in the conditional clause, especially after 'I'.

If I <u>were</u> as big as you, I would kill you.
If I <u>weren't</u> so busy, I would do it for you.

You often say 'If I were you' when you are giving someone advice.

> *If I were you, I would take the money.*
> *I should keep out of Bernadette's way*
> *if I were you.*

---

7 When you are talking about something which could have happened in the past but which did not actually happen, you use the past perfect in the conditional clause. In the main clause, you use 'would have' and an '-ed' participle.

> *If he had realized that, he would have run away.*
> *I wouldn't have been so depressed if I had known how common this feeling is.*

⚠ **BE CAREFUL**

You do not use 'would have' in the conditional clause. You do not say 'If I would have seen him, I would have told him'.

Unit 75: 'If' with modals; 'unless'

Main points

- You can use a modal in a conditional clause.
- You use 'unless' to mention an exception to what you are saying.

1   You sometimes use modals in conditional clauses. In the main clause, you can still use a present tense form for events that happen often, 'will' for events that are quite likely in the future, 'would' for an event that is unlikely to happen, and 'would have' for events that were possible but did not happen.

> If he _can't_ come, he usually _phones_ me.
> If they _must_ have it today, they _will_ have to come back at five o'clock.
> If I _could_ only find the time, I'_d_ do it gladly.
> If you _could have_ seen him, you _would have_ laughed too.

'Should' is sometimes used in conditional clauses to express greater uncertainty.

> If any visitors _should_ come, I'll say you aren't here.

292

2 You can use other modals besides 'will', 'would' and 'would have' in the main clause with their usual meanings.

> She <u>might</u> phone me, if she has time.
> You <u>could</u> come, if you wanted to.
> If he sees you leaving, he <u>may</u> cry.

Note that you can have modals in both clauses: the main clause and the conditional clause.

> If he <u>can't</u> come, he <u>will</u> phone.

3 In formal English, if the first verb in a conditional clause is 'had', 'should', or 'were', you can put the verb at the beginning of the clause and omit 'if'.

For example, instead of saying 'If he should come, I will tell him you are sick', it is possible to say 'Should he come, I will tell him you are sick'.

> <u>Should</u> ministers decide to hold an inquiry, we would welcome it.
> <u>Were</u> it all true, it would still not excuse their actions.
> <u>Had</u> I known, I would not have done it.

4 When you want to mention an exception to what you are saying, you use a conditional clause beginning with 'unless'.

You will fail your exams.
You will fail your exams <u>unless you work harder</u>.

Note that you can often use 'if...not' instead of 'unless'.

You will fail your exams <u>if</u> you do <u>not</u> work harder.

When you use 'unless', you use the same verb forms that you use with 'if'.

She <u>spends</u> Sundays in the garden unless the weather <u>is</u> awful.
We usually <u>walk</u>, unless we'<u>re going</u> shopping.
He <u>will</u> not <u>let</u> you go unless he <u>is forced</u> to do so.
You <u>wouldn't believe</u> it, unless you <u>saw</u> it.

5 'If' and 'unless' are not the only ways of beginning conditional clauses. You can also use 'as long as', 'only if', 'provided', 'provided that', 'providing', 'providing that', or 'so long as'. These expressions are all used to indicate that one thing only happens or is true if another thing happens or is true.

We were all right <u>as long as</u> we kept our heads down.
I will come <u>only if</u> nothing is said to the press.

She was prepared to come, <u>provided that</u> she could bring her daughter.

<u>Providing</u> they remained at a safe distance, we would be all right.

The system works well <u>providing that</u> you remember to take your passport with you.

Detergent cannot harm a fabric, <u>so long as</u> it has been properly dissolved.

Unit 76: I wish, if only, ...as if...

Main points

- You use 'I wish' and 'If only' to talk about wishes and regrets.
- You use '...as if...' and '...as though...' to show that information in a manner clause is not or might not be true.

1 You can express what you want to happen now by using 'I wish' or 'If only' followed by a past simple verb.

> _I wish_ he _wasn't_ here.
> _If only_ she _had_ a car.

Note that in formal English, you sometimes use 'were' instead of 'was' in sentences like these.

> _I often wish_ that I _were_ really wealthy.

When you want to express regret about past events, you use the past perfect.

> _I wish_ I _hadn't married_ him.

When you want to say that you wish that someone was able to do something, you use 'could'.

> _If only_ they _could_ come with us!

When you want to say that you wish that someone was willing to do something, you use 'would'.

> _If only_ they _would_ realise how stupid they've been.

2   When you want to indicate that the information in a manner clause might not be true, or is definitely not true, you use 'as if' or 'as though'.

> _She reacted as if she didn't know about the race._
> _She acts as though she owns the place._

After 'as if' or 'as though', you often use a past tense form even when you are talking about the present, to emphasize that the information in the manner clause is not true. In formal English, you use 'were' instead of 'was'.

> _Presidents can't dispose of companies as if people didn't exist._
> _She treats him as though he was her own son._
> _He looked at me as though I were mad._

3   You can also use 'as if' or 'as though' to say how someone or something feels, looks, or sounds.

> _She felt as if she had a fever._

He looked <u>as if</u> he hadn't slept very much.
Mary sounded <u>as though</u> she had just run all the way.

You can also use 'it looks' and 'it sounds' with 'as if' and 'as though'.

It looks to me <u>as if</u> he wrote down some notes.
It sounds to me <u>as though</u> he's just being awkward.

---

4 When the subject of the manner clause and the main clause are the same, you can often use a participle in the manner clause and omit the subject and the verb 'be'.

He ran off to the house <u>as if escaping</u>.
He shook his head <u>as though dazzled</u> by his own vision.

You can also use 'as if' or 'as though' with a 'to'-infinitive clause.

<u>As if to remind</u> him, the church clock struck eleven.

---

5 In informal speech, people often use 'like' instead of 'as if' or 'as' to say how a person feels, looks, or sounds. Some speakers of English think that this use of 'like' is incorrect.

He felt <u>like</u> he'd won the pools.
You look <u>like</u> you've seen a ghost.
You talk just <u>like</u> my father does.

You can also use 'like' in prepositional phrases to say how someone does something.

He was sleeping <u>like a baby</u>.
I behaved <u>like an idiot</u>, and I'm sorry.

Unit 77: Verbs with '-ing' clauses

Main points

- Many verbs are followed by an '-ing' clause.
- Some verbs are followed by an object and an '-ing' clause that describes what the object is doing.

1 Many verbs are followed by an '-ing' clause. The subject of the verb is also the subject of the '-ing' clause. The '-ing' clause begins with an '-ing' participle. The most common of these verbs are:

- verbs of saying and thinking

admit	consider	deny	describe
imagine	mention	recall	suggest

He <u>denied taking</u> drugs.
I <u>suggested meeting</u> her for a coffee.

- Note that all of these verbs except for 'describe' can also be followed by a 'that'-clause.
  → See Unit 84.

He <u>denied that</u> he was involved.

- verbs of liking and disliking

adore	detest	dislike	dread	enjoy
fancy	like	love	mind	resent

Will they <u>enjoy using</u> it?
I <u>don't mind telling</u> you.

- 'Like' and 'love' can also be followed by a 'to'-infinitive clause.
  → See Unit 79.

- other common verbs

avoid	commence	delay	finish
involve	keep	miss	postpone
practise	resist	risk	stop

I've just <u>finished reading</u> that book.
<u>Avoid giving</u> any unnecessary information.

- common phrasal verbs

burst out	carry on	end up	give up
go round	keep on	put off	set about

She <u>carried on reading</u>.
They <u>kept on walking</u> for a while.

- Note that some common phrases can be followed by an '-ing' clause.

can't help	can't stand	feel like

I <u>can't help worrying</u>.

2 After the verbs and phrases mentioned above, you can also use 'being' followed by an '-ed' participle.

> *They enjoy being praised.*
> *I dislike being interrupted.*

After some verbs of saying and thinking, you can use 'having' followed by an '-ed' participle.

admit	deny	mention	recall

> *Michael denied having seen him.*

3 'Come' and 'go' are used with '-ing' clauses to describe the way that a person or thing moves.

> *They both came running out.*
> *It went sliding across the road out of control.*

'Go' and 'come' are also used with '-ing' nouns to talk about sports and outdoor activities.

→ See Unit 64.

> *Did you say they might go camping?*

4 Some verbs can be followed by an object and an '-ing' clause. The object of the verb is the subject of the '-ing' clause.

catch	find	imagine	leave
prevent	stop	watch	

It is hard <u>to imagine him existing</u> without it.
He <u>left them making</u> their calculations.

Note that 'prevent' and 'stop' are often used with 'from' in front of the '-ing' clause.

I wanted to <u>prevent him from seeing</u> that.

Most verbs of perception can be followed by an object and an '-ing' clause or a base form.
→ See Unit 80.

I <u>saw him riding</u> a bicycle.
I <u>saw a policeman walk over</u> to one of them.

→ See also Unit 102 for '-ing' clauses after nouns.

Unit 78: Infinitives

Main points

- Some verbs are followed by a 'to'-infinitive clause. Others are followed by an object and a 'to'-infinitive clause.
- Some verbs are followed by a 'wh'-word and a 'to'-infinitive clause. Others are followed by an object, a 'wh'-word, and a 'to'-infinitive clause.
- Nouns are followed by 'to'-infinitive clauses that indicate the aim, purpose or necessity of something, or that give extra information.

1 Some verbs are followed by a 'to'-infinitive clause. The subject of the verb is also the subject of the 'to'-infinitive clause.

- verbs of saying and thinking

agree	choose	decide	expect
hope	intend	learn	mean
offer	plan	promise	refuse

She <u>had agreed to let</u> us use her flat for a while.
I <u>decided not to go out</u> for the evening.

- other verbs

fail	manage	pretend	tend	want

England <u>failed to win</u> a place in the European finals.

2 Some verbs are followed by an object and a 'to'-infinitive clause. The object of the verb is the subject of the 'to'-infinitive clause.

● verbs of saying and thinking

advise	ask	encourage	expect
invite	order	persuade	remind
teach	tell		

I <u>asked her to explain</u>.
They <u>advised us not to wait around</u> too much longer.

● other verbs

| allow | force | get | help | want |

I could <u>get someone else to do</u> it.
I <u>didn't want him to go</u>.

● Note that 'help' can also be followed by an object and a base form.

I <u>helped him fix</u> it.

⚠ BE CAREFUL

You do not use 'want' with a 'that'-clause. You do not say 'I want that you do something'.

3 Some verbs are followed by 'for' and an object, then a 'to'-infinitive clause. The object of 'for' is the subject of the 'to'-infinitive clause.

appeal	arrange	ask	long
pay	wait	wish	

Could you <u>arrange for a taxi to collect</u> us?
I <u>waited for him to speak</u>.

4 Some linking verbs, and 'pretend', are followed by 'to be' and an '-ing' participle for continuing actions, and by 'to have' and an '-ed' participle for finished actions.
→ See also Unit 62.

We <u>pretended to be looking</u> inside.
I <u>don't appear to have written down</u> his name.

5 Some verbs are normally used in the passive when they are followed by a 'to'-infinitive clause.

believe	consider	feel	find	know
report	say	think	understand	

He <u>is said to have died</u> a natural death.
<u>Is</u> it <u>thought to be</u> a good thing?

6 Some verbs are followed by a 'wh'-word and a 'to'-infinitive clause. These include:

ask	decide	explain	forget
imagine	know	learn	remember
understand	wonder		

I <u>didn't know what to call</u> him.
She <u>had forgotten how to ride</u> a bicycle.

Some verbs are followed by an object, then a 'wh'-word and a 'to'-infinitive clause.

| ask | remind | show | teach | tell |

I <u>asked him what to do</u>.
Who will <u>show him how to use</u> it?

Some verbs only take 'to'-infinitive clauses to express purpose.
→ See Unit 105.

The captain <u>stopped to reload</u> the gun.
He <u>went to get</u> some fresh milk.

7 You use a 'to'-infinitive clause after a noun phrase to indicate the aim of an action or the purpose of a physical object.

We arranged a meeting <u>to discuss the new rules</u>.
He had nothing <u>to write with</u>.

You also use a 'to'-infinitive clause after a noun phrase to say that something needs to be done.

> *I gave him several things <u>to mend</u>.*
> *'What's this?' – 'A list of things <u>to remember</u>.'*

8 You use a 'to'-infinitive clause after a noun phrase that includes an ordinal number, a superlative, or a word like 'next', 'last', or 'only'.

> *She was the <u>first</u> woman <u>to be elected to the council</u>.*
> *Mr Holmes was <u>the oldest</u> person <u>to be chosen</u>.*
> *The <u>only</u> person <u>to speak</u> was James.*

9 You use a 'to'-infinitive clause after abstract nouns to give more specific information about them.

> *All it takes is <u>a willingness to learn</u>.*
> *He lost <u>the ability to communicate</u> with people.*

The following abstract nouns are often followed by a 'to'-infinitive clause:

ability	attempt	chance
desire	failure	inability
need	opportunity	unwillingness
willingness		

Note that the verbs or adjectives which are related to these nouns can also be followed by a 'to'-infinitive clause. For example, you can say 'I attempted to find them', and 'He was willing to learn'.
→ See Unit 103 for information on nouns that are related to reporting verbs and can be followed by a 'to'-infinitive clause.

Unit 79: Verb + 'to' or '-ing'

Main point

Some verbs take a 'to'-infinitive clause or an '-ing' clause with little difference in meaning. Others take a 'to'-infinitive or '-ing' clause, but the meaning is different.

1 The following verbs can be followed by a 'to'-infinitive clause or an '-ing' clause, with little difference in meaning.

attempt	begin	bother	continue
fear	hate	love	prefer
start	try		

> It _started raining_.
> A very cold wind _had started to blow_.
> The captain _didn't bother answering_.
> I _didn't bother to answer_.

Note that if these verbs are used in the progressive, they are followed by a 'to'-infinitive clause.

> The company _is beginning to export_ to the West.
> We _are continuing to make_ good progress.

After 'begin', 'continue', and 'start', you use a 'to'-infinitive clause with the verbs 'understand', 'know', and 'realize'.

> I <u>began to understand</u> her a bit better.

2 You can often use 'like' with a 'to'-infinitive or an '-ing' clause with little difference in meaning.

> I <u>like to fish</u>.
> I <u>like fishing</u>.

However, there is sometimes a difference. You can use 'like' followed by a 'to'-infinitive clause to say that you think something is a good idea, or the right thing to do. You cannot use an '-ing' clause with this meaning.

> They <u>like to interview</u> people first.
> I <u>didn't like to ask</u> him.

3 After 'remember', 'forget', and 'regret', you use an '-ing' clause if you are referring to an event after it has happened.

> I <u>remember discussing</u> it once before.
> I'll never <u>forget seeing</u> the Taj Mahal.
> She did not <u>regret accepting</u> his offer.

You use a 'to'-infinitive clause after 'remember' and 'forget' if you are referring to an event before it happens.

I must <u>remember to call</u> Dad tonight.
Don't <u>forget to send in</u> your entries.

After 'regret', in formal English, you use a 'to'-infinitive clause with these verbs to say that you are sorry about what you are saying or doing now:

| announce | inform | learn | say | see | tell |

We <u>regret to announce</u> that the London train has been cancelled.

---

4 If you 'try to do' something, you make an effort to do it. If you 'try doing' something, you do it as an experiment, for example to see if you like it or if it is effective.

I <u>tried to explain</u>.

---

5 If you 'go on doing' something, you continue to do it. If you 'go on to do' something, you do it after you have finished doing something else.

I <u>went on writing</u>.
He later <u>went on to form</u> a computer company.

---

6 If you 'are used to doing' something, you are accustomed to doing it. If you 'used to do' something, you did it regularly in the past, but you no longer do it now.

We <u>are used to working</u> together.
I <u>used to live</u> in this street.

7 After 'need', you use a 'to'-infinitive clause
   if the subject of 'need' is also the subject
   of the 'to'-infinitive clause. You use an '-ing'
   participle if the subject of 'need' is the
   object of the '-ing' clause.

   We <u>need to ask</u> certain questions.
   It <u>needs cutting</u>.

Unit 80: Verbs with other clauses

Main points

- 'Make' and 'let' can be followed by an object and a base form.
- Some verbs of perception can be followed by an object and an '-ing' clause, or an object and a base form.
- 'Have' and 'get' can be followed by an object and an '-ed' participle.
- 'Dare' is followed by a 'to'-infinitive clause or a base form.

1 You can use an object and a base form after 'make' to say that one person causes another person to do something, or after 'let' to say they allow them to do something.

> My father <u>made me go</u> for the interview.
> Jenny <u>let him talk</u>.

2 Some verbs of perception are used with an object and an '-ing' clause if an action is unfinished or continues over a period of time, and with an object and a base form if the action is finished.

| feel | hear | see | watch |

He <u>heard a distant voice shouting</u>.
Dr Hochstadt <u>heard her gasp</u>.

You normally use an '-ing' clause after 'notice', 'observe', 'smell', and 'understand'.

I didn't <u>notice her leaving</u>.
We can <u>understand them wanting</u> to go.

3 You can use an object and an '-ed' participle after 'have' or 'get', when you want to say that someone arranges for something to be done. 'Have' is slightly more formal.

We've just <u>had the house decorated</u>.
We must <u>get the car repaired</u>.

You also use 'have' and 'get' with an object and an '-ed' participle to say that something happens to someone, especially if it is unpleasant.

She <u>had her purse stolen</u>.
He <u>got his car broken into</u> at the weekend.

4 You use 'have' followed by an object and an '-ing' clause, or an object and an '-ed' participle, when you want to say that someone causes something to happen, either intentionally or unintentionally.

Alan had me looking for that book all day.
He had me utterly confused.

---

5 You use 'want' and 'would like' with an object and an '-ed' participle to indicate that you want something to be done.

I want the work finished by January 1st.
How would you like your hair cut, sir?

---

6 'Dare' can be followed by a 'to'-infinitive clause or a base form in negative or interrogative sentences:

- when there is an auxiliary or modal before 'dare'

He did not dare to walk to the village.
What bank would dare offer such terms?

- when you use the form 'dares' or 'dared' (but not 'dares not' or 'dared not')

No one dares disturb him.
No other manager dared to compete.

You must use a base form in:

- negative or interrogative sentences without an auxiliary or modal before 'dare'

I daren't ring Jeremy again.
Nobody dare disturb him.
Dare she go in?

- negative sentences with 'dares not' or 'dared not'

  He <u>dares not risk</u> it.
  Sonny <u>dared not disobey</u>.

Note that the phrase 'how dare you' is always followed by a base form.

  How <u>dare</u> you <u>speak</u> to me like that?

'Dare' is rarely used in affirmative sentences.

Unit 81: Direct speech

Main points

- When you use direct speech, you report what someone said as if you were using their own words.
- Direct speech consists of two clauses: a reporting clause and a quote.
- The reporting clause contains a reporting verb such as 'say', 'ask', or 'explain'.
- The quote represents what someone says. It starts and ends with quotation marks.
- The reporting clause is usually put after the quote.

1 You can use either direct speech or reported speech to report what someone said.

When you use direct speech, you report what someone said as if you were using their own words. Direct speech is more often used in stories than in ordinary conversation.

   'It's time to go', said Katrina.

When you use reported speech, you report

what someone said in your own words.

Katrina said it was time to go.

2 Direct speech consists of two clauses. One clause is the reporting clause, which contains the reporting verb.

Here are some common reporting verbs:

agree	answer	ask	explain
inquire	promise	remark	reply
say	suggest	tell	wonder

Other reporting verbs show how something was said, such as 'shout', 'whisper', and 'mutter'.

'Sorry I'm late,' <u>she said</u>.
'Yes please,' <u>replied John</u>.
'Where are we?' <u>I whispered</u>.

3 The other clause is the quote, which represents what someone said.

In writing, you use quotation marks (' ') or (" ") at the beginning and end of a quote.

The quote begins with a capital letter, and it is separated from the reporting clause with a comma, unless the quote ends with a question mark or an exclamation mark.

<u>'Let's go and have a look at the</u>

swimming pool,' she suggested.
"_Leave me alone!_" I shouted.

---

4 You can also use direct speech to represent what someone thinks, using reporting verbs like 'think' and 'wonder'.

When you are using direct speech to represent what someone thinks, you usually omit the quotation marks.

I must call Dad, Martha thought.
Why, she wondered, was he working so late?

---

5 The reporting clause is usually put after the quote.

'_You have to keep trying,_' he said.

It can also be put in the middle of the quote, at a natural pause.

'_You see,_' he explained, '_my father was a doctor._'

Some reporting verbs can be put in front of the quote.

She hugged him and said, 'It's great to see you.'

Note that the reporting verbs 'agree', 'promise', and 'wonder' are hardly ever used in front of a quote.

6 When a reporting clause comes after a quote, the subject is often put after the verb if the subject is a noun.

> *'That's a good idea,' <u>remarked Dave</u>.*
> *'Are you ready to order?' <u>asked the waiter</u>.*

If the subject is a pronoun, it is put in front of the verb.

> *'Are you ready to order?' <u>he asked</u>.*

Unit 82: Reported speech

Main points

- You use reported speech to report what people say or think in your own words.
- You use the present tense of the reporting verb when you are reporting something that someone says or thinks at the time you are speaking.
- You often use past tense forms in reporting structures because a reported clause usually reports something that was said or believed in the past.

1 You use reported speech to report what people say or think in your own words.

> *Jim said he wanted to go home.*

Jim's actual words might have been 'It's time I went' or 'I must go'.

Reported speech consists of two parts. One part is the reporting clause, which contains the reporting verb.

> <u>*I told him*</u> *nothing was going to happen to me.*
> <u>*I agreed*</u> *that he should do it.*

The other part is the reported clause.

He felt <u>that he had to do something</u>.
Henry said <u>he wanted to go home</u>.

2 For the verb in the reporting clause, you choose a verb form that is appropriate at the time you are speaking.

Because reports are usually about something that was said or believed in the past, both the reporting verb and the verb in the reported clause are often in a past tense form.

Mrs Kaur <u>announced</u> that the lecture <u>had begun</u>.
At the time we <u>thought</u> that he <u>was</u> mad.

3 Although you normally use past tense forms in reports about the past, you can use a present tense form in the reported clause if what you are saying is important in the present, for example:

• because you want to emphasize that it is still true

<u>Did</u> you <u>tell</u> him that this young woman <u>is looking</u> for a job?

• because you want to give advice or a warning, or make a suggestion for the present or future

*I <u>told</u> you they <u>have</u> this class on Friday
afternoon, so you should have come a
bit earlier.*

---

4 You use a present tense form for the
reporting verb when you are reporting:

- what someone says or thinks at the
  time you are speaking

  *She <u>says</u> she wants to see you in her office
  this afternoon.*
  *I <u>think</u> there's something wrong with the
  central heating system.*

Note that, as in the last example, it may
be your own thoughts that you are
reporting.

- what someone often says

  He <u>says</u> that no one understands him.
  *She <u>tells</u> everyone that she is going to live in
  America.*

- what someone has said in the past,
  if what they said is still true

  My doctor <u>says</u> it's nothing to worry about.
  *Freud <u>says</u> that experiences in later life may
  be healing.*

---

5 If you are predicting what people will say
or think, you use a future form for the
reporting verb.

*No doubt he <u>will claim</u> that his car
broke down.*
They <u>will think</u> we are making a fuss.

Unit 83: Reported questions

Main points

- You use reported questions to talk about a question that someone else has asked.
- In reported questions, the subject of the question comes before the verb.
- You use 'if' or 'whether' in reported 'yes/no'-questions.

1   When you are talking about a question that someone has asked, you use a reported question.

> She asked me <u>why I was so late</u>.
> He wanted to know <u>where I was going</u>.
> I demanded to know <u>what was going on</u>.
> I asked her <u>if I could help her</u>.
> I asked her <u>whether there was anything wrong</u>.

In formal and written English, 'enquire' (also spelled 'inquire') is often used instead of 'ask'.

> MrWilkie had enquired <u>if she did a lot of acting</u>.
> He inquired <u>whether he could see her</u>.

2 When you are reporting a question, the verb in the reported clause is often in a past tense form. This is because you are often talking about the past when you are reporting someone else's words.

> *She <u>asked</u> me why I <u>was</u> so late.*
> *Pat <u>asked</u> him if she <u>had hurt</u> him.*

However, you can use a present or future form if the question you are reporting relates to the present or future.

> *Mark <u>was asking</u> if you<u>'re enjoying</u> your new job.*
> *They <u>asked</u> if you<u>'ll be</u> there tomorrow night.*

3 In reported questions, the subject of the question comes before the verb, just as it does in affirmative sentences.

> *She asked me why <u>I was late</u>.*
> *I asked what <u>he was doing</u>.*

4 You do not normally use the auxiliary 'do' in reported questions.

> *She asked him if <u>his parents spoke</u> French or German.*
> *They asked us what <u>we thought</u>.*

The auxiliary 'do' can be used in reported questions, but only for emphasis, or to make a contrast with something that has already been said. It is not put before the subject as in direct questions.

She asked me whether I really <u>did</u> mean what I'd said.
I told him I didn't like classical music. He asked me what kind of music I <u>did</u> like.

---

5 You use 'if' or 'whether' to introduce reported 'yes/no'-questions.

I asked him <u>if</u> he was on holiday.
The bride's mother asked me <u>if</u> anything was wrong.
She hugged him and asked him <u>whether</u> he was all right.
I asked him <u>whether</u> he was single.

'Whether' is used especially when there is a choice of possibilities.

I was asked <u>whether</u> I wanted to stay at a hotel <u>or</u> at his home.
They asked <u>whether</u> Tim was <u>or</u> was not in the team.
I asked him <u>whether</u> he loved me <u>or</u> not.

Note that you can put 'or not' immediately after 'whether', but not immediately after 'if'.

The police didn't ask <u>whether or not</u> they were in.

→ See Units 82, 84, and 85 for more
information on reporting.

Unit 84: Reported speech: 'that'-clauses

Main points

- Reported speech contains a reporting clause first, then a reported clause.
- When you are reporting a statement, the reported clause is a 'that'-clause.
- You must mention the hearer with 'tell'. You need not mention the hearer with 'say'.

1 Reported speech contains two clauses. The first clause is the reporting clause, which contains a reporting verb such as 'say', 'tell', or 'ask'.

> _She said_ that she'd been to Belgium.
> _The man in the shop told me_ how much it would cost.

You often use verbs that refer to people's thoughts and feelings to report what people say. If someone says 'I am wrong', you might report this as 'He felt that he was wrong'.
→ See Unit 77.

2 The second clause is the reported clause, which contains the information that you are reporting. The reported clause can be a 'that'-clause, a 'to'-infinitive clause, an 'if'-clause, or a 'wh'-word clause.

> She said <u>that she didn't know</u>.
> He told me <u>to do it</u>.
> Mary asked <u>if she could stay with us</u>.
> She asked <u>where he'd gone</u>.

3 If you want to report a statement, you use a 'that'-clause after a verb such as 'say'.

admit	agree	answer	argue
claim	complain	decide	deny
explain	insist	mention	promise
reply	say	warn	

> He <u>said that</u> he would go.
> I <u>replied that</u> I had not read it yet.

You often omit 'that' from the 'that'-clause, but not after 'answer', 'argue', 'explain', or 'reply'.

> They <u>said</u> I had to see a doctor first.
> He <u>answered that</u> the price could not be changed.

You often mention the hearer after the preposition 'to' with the following verbs.

| admit | announce | complain | explain |
| mention | say | | suggest |

He <u>complained to me</u> *that you were rude.*

---

4 'Tell' and some other reporting verbs are also used with a 'that'-clause, but with these verbs you have to mention the hearer as the object of the verb.

| convince | inform | notify | persuade |
| reassure | remind | tell | |

He <u>told me</u> *that he was a farmer.*
I <u>informed her</u> *that I could not come.*

The word 'that' is often omitted after 'tell'.

I <u>told them</u> *you were at the dentist.*

You can also mention the hearer as the object of the verb with 'promise' and 'warn'.

I <u>promised her</u> *that I wouldn't be late.*

---

5 Note the differences between 'say' and 'tell'. You cannot use 'say' with the hearer as the object of the verb. You cannot say 'I said them you had gone'. You cannot use 'tell' without the hearer as the object of the verb. You cannot say 'I told that you had gone'. You cannot use 'tell' with 'to' and the hearer. You cannot say 'I told to them you had gone'.

6 The reporting verbs that have the hearer as object, such as 'tell', can be used in the passive.

She <u>was told</u> that there were no tickets left.

Most reporting verbs that do not need the hearer as object, such as 'say', can be used in the passive with impersonal 'it' as subject, but not 'answer', 'complain', 'insist', 'promise', 'reply', or 'warn'.

<u>It was said</u> that the money had been stolen.

→ See also Units 82 and 85.

Unit 85: Other reporting structures

Main points

- When reporting an order, a request, or a piece of advice, the reported clause is a 'to'-infinitive clause, used after an object.
- When reporting a question, the reported clause is an 'if'-clause or a 'wh'-word clause.
- Many reporting verbs refer to people's thoughts and feelings.

1 If you want to report an order, a request, or a piece of advice, you use a 'to'-infinitive clause after a reporting verb such as 'tell', 'ask', or 'advise'. You mention the hearer as the object of the verb, before the 'to'-infinitive clause.

advise	ask	beg	command
forbid	instruct	invite	order
persuade	remind	tell	warn

Johnson <u>told her to wake</u> him up.
He <u>ordered me to fetch</u> the books.

He <u>asked her to marry</u> him.
He <u>advised me to buy</u> it.

If the order, request, or advice is negative, you put 'not' before the 'to'-infinitive.

He had ordered his officers <u>not to use</u> any weapons.
She asked her staff <u>not to discuss</u> it publicly.
Doctors advised him <u>not to play</u> for three weeks.

If the subject of the 'to'-infinitive clause is the same as the subject of the main verb, you can use 'ask' or 'beg' to report a request without mentioning the hearer.

I <u>asked to see</u> the manager.
Both men <u>begged not to be named</u>.

2 If you want to report a question, you use a verb such as 'ask' followed by an 'if'-clause or a 'wh'-word clause.

I <u>asked if</u> I could stay with them.
They <u>wondered whether</u> the time was right.
He <u>asked</u> me <u>where</u> I was going.
She <u>inquired how</u> Ibrahim was getting on.

Note that in reported questions, the subject of the question comes before the verb, just as it does in affirmative sentences.
→ See Unit 83.

3 Many reporting verbs refer to people's thoughts and feelings but are often used to report what people say. For example, if someone says 'I must go', you might report this as 'She wanted to go' or 'She thought she should go'.

Some of these verbs are followed by:

• a 'that'-clause

accept	believe	consider	fear
feel	guess	imagine	know
suppose	think	understand	worry

We both <u>knew</u> that the town was cut off.
I had always <u>believed</u> that I would see him again.

• a 'to'-infinitive clause

| intend | plan | want |

We <u>plan to</u> open a second restaurant near Hopkinsville.
He doesn't <u>want</u> to get up.

• a 'that'-clause or a 'to'-infinitive clause

| agree | decide | expect | | forget | hope |
| prefer | regret | remember | wish | | |

She <u>hoped she wasn't going to cry</u>.
They are in love and <u>wish to marry</u>.

'Expect' and 'prefer' can also be followed by an object and a 'to'-infinitive.

> I'm sure she <u>doesn't expect you to take</u> the plane.
> The headmaster <u>prefers them to act</u> plays they have written themselves.

Unit 86: The passive

Main points

- You use the passive to focus on the person or thing affected by an action.
- You form the passive by using a form of 'be' and an '-ed' participle.
- Only verbs that have an object can have a passive form. With verbs that can have two objects, either object can be the subject of the passive.

1 When you want to talk about the person or thing that performs an action, you use the active.

> Mr Smith <u>locks</u> the gate at 6 o'clock every night.
> The storm <u>destroyed</u> dozens of trees.

When you want to focus on the person or thing that is affected by an action, rather than the person or thing that performs the action, you use the passive.

> The gate <u>is locked</u> at 6 o'clock every night.
> Dozens of trees <u>were destroyed</u>.

2 The passive is formed with a form of the auxiliary 'be', followed by the '-ed' participle of a main verb.

> *Two new stores <u>were opened</u> this year.*
> *The room <u>had been cleaned</u>.*

Progressive passives are formed with a form of the auxiliary 'be' followed by 'being' and the '-ed' participle of a main verb.

> *Jobs <u>are</u> still <u>being lost</u>.*
> *It <u>was being done</u> without his knowledge.*

3 After modals you use the base form 'be' followed by the '-ed' participle of a main verb.

> *What <u>can be done</u>?*
> *We <u>won't be beaten</u>.*

When you are talking about the past, you use a modal with 'have been' followed by the '-ed' participle of a main verb.

> *He <u>may have been given</u> the car.*
> *He <u>couldn't have been told</u> by Jimmy.*

4 You form passive infinitives by using 'to be' or 'to have been' followed by the '-ed' participle of a main verb.

> *He wanted <u>to be forgiven</u>.*
> *The car was reported <u>to have been stolen</u>.*

5 In informal English, 'get' is sometimes used instead of 'be' to form the passive.

> Our car <u>gets cleaned</u> every weekend.
> He <u>got killed</u> in a plane crash.

---

6 When you use the passive, you often do not mention the person or thing that performs the action at all. This may be because you do not know or do not want to say who it is, or because it does not matter.

> Her boyfriend <u>was shot</u> in the chest.
> Your application <u>was rejected</u>.
> Such items should <u>be</u> carefully <u>packed</u> in boxes.

---

7 If you are using the passive and you do want to mention the person or thing that performs or causes the action, you use 'by'.

> He was brought up <u>by</u> an aunt.
> The flood was caused <u>by</u> a burst pipe.

You use 'with' to talk about something that is used to perform the action.

> A circle was drawn in the dirt <u>with</u> a stick.
> He was killed <u>with</u> a knife.

---

8 Only verbs that usually have an object can have a passive form. For example, you can say 'people spend money' or 'money is spent'.

*An enormous amount of money <u>is spent</u>
on advertising.*
The food <u>is sold</u> at local markets.

With verbs which can have two objects,
you can form two different passive
sentences. For example, you can say
'The secretary was given the key' or
'The key was given to the secretary'.

They <u>were offered</u> a new flat.
The books <u>will be sent</u> to you.

→ See Unit 59 for more information on
verbs that can have two objects.

Unit 87: Introduction to modals

Main points

- The modal verbs are: 'can', 'could', 'may', 'might', 'must', 'ought', 'shall', 'should', 'will', and 'would'.
- Modals are always the first word in a verb phrase.
- All modals except for 'ought' are followed by the base form of a verb.
- 'Ought' is followed by a 'to'-infinitive.
- Modals have only one form.

1   The modal verbs are: 'can', 'could', 'may', 'might', 'must', 'ought', 'shall', 'should', 'will', and 'would'.

Modals are always the first word in a verb phrase. All modals except for 'ought' are followed by the base form of a verb.

> I _must leave_ fairly soon.
> I think it _will look_ rather nice.
> Things _might have been_ so different.
> People _may be watching_.
> She _can speak_ Spanish.
> I wonder if I _could ask_ you a question.

I <u>shall arrive</u> before sunset.
Nobody <u>will remember</u> what you said.

---

2 'Ought' is always followed by a 'to'-infinitive.

She <u>ought to go</u> straight back to New Zealand.
Sam <u>ought to have realized</u> how dangerous it was.
You <u>ought to be doing</u> this.

---

3 Modals have only one form. There is no '-s' form for the third person singular of the present tense, and there are no '-ing' or '-ed' forms.

There's nothing <u>I can</u> do about it.
I'm sure <u>he can</u> do it.
<u>You must</u> see the painting he has given me.
<u>She must</u> have a good idea what is happening.
<u>We should</u> talk about it at dinner tonight.
<u>The parcel should</u> arrive no later than tomorrow.

---

4 Modals do not normally indicate the time when something happens. There are, however, a few exceptions.

'Shall' and 'will' often indicate a future event or situation.

I <u>shall</u> do what you suggested.
He <u>will</u> not return for many hours.

'Could' is used as the past form of 'can' to express ability. 'Would' is used as the past form of 'will' to express the future.

When I was young, I <u>could</u> run for miles and miles.
He remembered that he <u>would</u> see his mother the next day.

5 In spoken English and informal written English, 'shall' and 'will' are shortened to '-'ll', and 'would' to '-'d', and added to a pronoun.

<u>I'll</u> see you tomorrow.
I hope <u>you'll</u> agree.
Sandra said <u>she'd</u> love to stay.

'Shall', 'will', and 'would' are never shortened if they come at the end of a sentence.

Paul promised that he would come, and I hope he <u>will</u>.
I'm doing exactly what I said I <u>would</u>.

In spoken English, you can also add '-'ll' and '-'d' to nouns.

My <u>car'll</u> be outside.
The <u>headmaster'd</u> be furious if he found out about it.

⚠ BE CAREFUL

Remember that '-'d' is also the short form of the auxiliary 'had'.

I'<u>d</u> heard it many times.

Unit 88: Modals: negation, questions

Main points

- You use negative words with modals to make negative clauses.
- Modals go in front of the subject in questions.
- You never use two modals together.

1 To make a clause negative, you put a negative word immediately after the modal.

> You <u>must not</u> worry.
> I <u>can never</u> remember his name.
> He <u>ought not</u> to have done that.

'Can not' is always written as one word, 'cannot'.

> I <u>cannot</u> go back.

However, if 'can' is followed by 'not only', 'can' and 'not' are not joined.

> We <u>can not only</u> book your flight for you, but also advise you about hotels.

2 In spoken English and informal written English, 'not' is often shortened to '-n't' and added to the modal. The following modals are often shortened in this way:

could not:	couldn't
should not:	shouldn't
must not:	mustn't
would not:	wouldn't

> We <u>couldn't</u> leave the farm.
> You <u>mustn't</u> talk about Ron like that.
> I <u>shouldn't</u> have said what I did.

Note the following irregular short forms:

shall not:	shan't
will not:	won't
cannot:	can't

> I <u>shan't</u> let you go.
> <u>Won't</u> you change your mind?
> We <u>can't</u> stop now.

'Might not' and 'ought not' are sometimes shortened to 'mightn't' and 'oughtn't'.

> He <u>mightn't</u> be back until tonight.
> Perhaps I <u>oughtn't</u> to interfere.

Note that 'may not' is very rarely shortened to 'mayn't' in modern English.

3 To make a question, you put the modal in front of the subject.

> _Could you_ give me an example?
> _Will you_ be coming in later?
> _Shall I_ shut the door?

Modals are also used in question tags.
→ See Units 7 and 8 for more information.

---

4 You never use two modals together. For example, you cannot say 'He will can come'. Instead you can say 'He will be able to come'.

> I _shall have to_ go.
> Your husband _might have to_ give up work.

---

5 Instead of using modals, you can often use other verbs and expressions to make requests, offers, or suggestions, to express wishes or intentions, or to show that you are being polite.

For example, 'be able to' is used instead of 'can', 'be likely to' is used instead of 'might', and 'have to' is used instead of 'must'.

> All members _are able to_ claim expenses.
> I think that we _are likely to_ see more of this.

These expressions are also used after modals.

> *I really thought I <u>wouldn't be able to</u> visit you this week.*

---

6 'Dare' and 'need' sometimes behave like modals.
→ See Unit 80 for information on 'dare' and Units 79 and 98 for information on 'need'.

Unit 89: Possibility

Main points

- You use 'can' to say that something is possible.
- You use 'could', 'might', and 'may' to indicate that you are not certain whether something is possible, but you think it is.

1 When you want to say that something is possible, you use 'can'.

Cooking <u>can</u> be a real pleasure.
In some cases this <u>can</u> cause difficulty.

You use 'cannot' or 'can't' to say that something is not possible.

This <u>cannot</u> be the answer.
You <u>can't</u> be serious.

2 When you want to indicate that you are not certain whether something is possible, but you think it is, you use 'could', 'might', or 'may'. There is no important difference in meaning between these modals, but 'may' is slightly more formal.

That <u>could</u> be one reason.
He <u>might</u> come.
They <u>may</u> help us.

You can also use 'might not' or 'may not' in this way.

> *He <u>might not</u> be in England at all.*
> *They <u>may not</u> get a house with central heating.*

Note that 'could not' normally refers to ability in the past.
→ See Unit 91.

3 When there is a possibility that something happened in the past, but you are not certain if it actually happened, you use 'could have', 'may have', or 'might have', followed by an '-ed' participle.

> *It <u>could have been</u> tomato soup.*
> *You <u>may have noticed</u> this advertisement.*

You can also use 'might not have' or 'may not have' in this way.

> *He <u>might not have seen</u> me.*
> *They <u>may not have done</u> it.*

You use 'could not have' when you want to indicate that it is not possible that something happened.

> *He didn't have a boat, so he <u>couldn't have rowed</u> away.*
> *It <u>couldn't have been</u> wrong.*

You also use 'could have' to say that there was a possibility of something happening in the past, but it did not happen.

> It _could have been_ awful. (But it wasn't awful.)
> You _could have got_ a job last year.
> (But you didn't get a job.)

4 You also use 'might have' or 'could have' followed by an '-ed' participle to say that if a particular thing had happened, then there was a possibility of something else happening.

> She said it _might have been_ all right, if the weather had been good. (But the weather wasn't good, so it wasn't all right.)
> If I'd been there, I _could have helped_ you. (But I wasn't there, so I couldn't help you.)

5 'Be able to', 'not be able to', and 'be unable to' are sometimes used instead of 'can' and 'cannot', for example after another modal, or when you want to use a 'to'-infinitive, an '-ing' participle, or an '-ed' participle.

> When _will I be able to_ pick them up?
> We hope _to be able to_ announce the decision next week.
> I remember _not being able to_ swim.
> He had _been unable to_ get a ticket.

6 You use 'used to be able to' to say that something was possible in the past, but is not possible now.

> *Children <u>used to be able to</u> play in the streets, but it's too dangerous now.*
> *I <u>used to be able to</u> talk to him about anything.*

7 Note that you also use 'could' followed by a negative word and the comparative form of an adjective to emphasize a quality that someone or something has. For example, if you say 'I couldn't be happier', you mean that you are very happy indeed and cannot imagine being happier than you are now.

> *You <u>couldn't</u> be <u>more wrong</u>.*
> *He <u>could hardly</u> have felt <u>more ashamed</u> of himself.*

Unit 90: Probability and certainty

Main points

- You use 'must', 'ought', 'should', or 'will' to express probability or certainty.
- You use 'cannot' or 'can't' as the negative of 'must', rather than 'must not' or 'mustn't', to say that something is not probable or is not certain.

1 When you want to say that something is probably true or that it will probably happen, you use 'should' or 'ought'. 'Should' is followed by the base form of a verb. 'Ought' is followed by a 'to'-infinitive.

   We <u>should</u> arrive by dinner time.
   She <u>ought</u> to know.

   When you want to say that you think something is probably not true or that it will probably not happen, you use 'should not' or 'ought not'.

   There <u>shouldn't</u> be any problem.
   That <u>ought not</u> to be too difficult.

2 When you want to say that you are fairly sure that something has happened, you use 'should have' or 'ought to have', followed by an '-ed' participle.

> You _should have_ heard by now that I'm O.K.
> They _ought to have_ arrived yesterday.

When you want to say that you do not think that something has happened, you use 'should not have' or 'ought not to have', followed by an '-ed' participle.

> They _shouldn't have_ had any difficulty in getting here.
> This _ought not to have_ been a problem.

3 You also use 'should have' or 'ought to have' to say that you expected something to happen, but that it did not happen.

> Yesterday _should have been_ the start of the soccer season.
> She _ought to have been_ home by now.

Note that you do not normally use the negative forms with this meaning.

4 When you are fairly sure that something is the case, you use 'must'.

> Oh, you _must_ be Sylvia's husband.
> He _must_ know something about it.

If you are fairly sure that something is not the case, you use 'cannot' or 'can't'.

> *This <u>cannot</u> be the whole story.*
> *He <u>can't</u> be very old – he's about 25, isn't he?*

⚠ BE CAREFUL

You do not use 'must not' or 'mustn't' with this meaning.

---

5 When you want to say that you are almost certain that something has happened, you use 'must have', followed by an '-ed' participle.

> *This article <u>must have been</u> written by a woman.*
> *We <u>must have taken</u> the wrong road.*

To say that you do not think that something has happened, you use 'can't have', followed by an '-ed' participle.

> *You <u>can't have forgotten</u> me.*
> *He <u>can't have said</u> that.*

---

6 You use 'will' or '-'ll' to say that something is certain to happen in the future.

> *People <u>will</u> always say things you want to hear.*
> *They'<u>ll</u> manage.*

You use 'will not' or 'won't' to say that something is certain not to happen.

You <u>won't</u> get much sympathy from them.

7 There are several ways of talking about probability and certainty without using modals. For example, you can use:

- 'bound to' followed by the base form of a verb

  It was <u>bound to</u> happen.
  You're <u>bound to</u> make a mistake.

- an adjective such as 'certain', 'likely', 'sure', or 'unlikely', followed by a 'to'-infinitive clause or a 'that'-clause

  They were <u>certain</u> that you would lose.
  I am not <u>likely</u> to forget it.

→ See Unit 38 for more information on these adjectives.

Unit 91: Ability

Main points

- You use 'can' to talk about ability in the present and in the future.
- You use 'could' to talk about ability in the past.
- You use 'be able to' to talk about ability in the present, future, and past.

1 You use 'can' to say that someone has the ability to do something.

> You _can_ all read and write.
> Anybody _can_ become a qualified teacher.

You use 'cannot' or 'can't' to say that they do not have the ability to do something.

> He _cannot_ dance.
> I _can't_ speak German.

2 When you want to talk about someone's ability in the past as a result of a skill they had or did not have, you use 'could', 'could not', or 'couldn't'.

> He _could_ run faster than anyone else.
> A lot of them _couldn't_ read or write.

3 You also use 'be able to', 'not be able to', and 'be unable to' to talk about someone's ability to do something, but 'can' and 'could' are more common.

> *She was able to tie her own shoelaces.*
> *They are not able to run very fast.*
> *Many people were unable to read or write.*

---

4 You use a past form of 'be able to' to say that someone managed to do something in a particular situation in the past.

> *After treatment he was able to return to work.*
> *The farmers were able to pay the new wages.*
> *We were able to find time to discuss it.*

⚠ BE CAREFUL

You do not normally use 'could' to say that someone managed to do something in a particular situation. However, you can use 'could not' or 'couldn't' to say that someone did not manage to do something in a particular situation.

> *We couldn't stop laughing.*
> *I just couldn't think of anything to say.*

---

5 When you want to say that someone had the ability to do something in the past, but did not do it, you use 'could have' followed by an '-ed' participle.

> *You could have given it all to me.*

You know, she <u>could have done</u> French.

You often use this form when you want to express disapproval about something that was not done.

You <u>could have been</u> a little bit tidier.
You <u>could have told</u> me!

---

6 You use 'could not have' or 'couldn't have' followed by an '-ed' participle to say that it is not possible that someone had the ability to do something.

I <u>couldn't have gone</u> with you, because I was in London at the time.
She <u>couldn't have taken</u> the car, because Jim was using it.

---

7 In most cases, you can choose to use 'can' or 'be able to'. However, you sometimes have to use 'be able to'. You have to use 'be able to' if you are using another modal, or if you want to use an '-ing' participle, an '-ed' participle, or a 'to'-infinitive.

Nobody else <u>will be able</u> to read it.
...the satisfaction of <u>being able to</u> do the job.
I don't think I'd have <u>been able to</u> get an answer.
You're foolish to expect <u>to be able to</u> do that.

8 You also use 'can' or 'could' with verbs such as 'see', 'hear', and 'smell' to say that someone is or was aware of something through one of their senses.

> I <u>can smell</u> gas.
> I <u>can't see</u> her.
> I <u>could see</u> a few stars in the sky.
> There was such a noise we <u>couldn't hear</u>.

Unit 92: Permission

Main points

- You use 'can' or 'be allowed to' to talk about whether someone has permission to do something or not.

- You usually use 'can' to give someone permission to do something.

- You usually use 'can' or 'could' to ask for permission to do something.

1 You use 'can' to say that someone is allowed to do something. You use 'cannot' or 'can't' to say that they are not allowed to do it.

> Students <u>can</u> take a year away from university.
> Children <u>cannot</u> swim except in the presence of two lifeguards.

You use 'could' to say that someone was allowed to do something in the past. You use 'could not' or 'couldn't' to say that they were not allowed to do it.

> They <u>could</u> go to any part of the island they wanted.

Both students and staff <u>could</u> use the swimming pool.
We <u>couldn't</u> go into the library after 5 pm.

---

2 You also use 'be allowed to' when you are talking about permission, but not when you are asking for it or giving it.

When Mr Wilt asks for a solicitor he will <u>be allowed to</u> see one.
It was only after several months that I <u>was allowed to</u> visit her.
You<u>'re</u> not <u>allowed to</u> use calculators in exams.

---

3 In more formal situations, 'may' is used to say that someone is allowed to do something, and 'may not' is used to say that they are not allowed to do it.

They <u>may</u> do exactly as they like.
The retailer <u>may not</u> sell that book below the publisher's price.

---

4 When you want to give someone permission to do something, you use 'can'.

You <u>can</u> borrow that pen if you want to.
You <u>can</u> go off duty now.
She <u>can</u> go with you.

'May' is also used to give permission, but this is more formal.

> *You <u>may</u> speak.*
> *You <u>may</u> leave as soon as you have finished.*

---

5 When you want to refuse someone permission to do something, you use 'cannot', 'can't', 'will not', 'won't', 'shall not', or 'shan't'.

> *'Can I have some sweets?' – 'No, you <u>can't</u>!'*
> *'I'll just go upstairs.' – 'You <u>will not</u>!'*
> *You <u>shan't</u> leave without my permission.*

---

6 When you are asking for permission to do something, you use 'can' or 'could'. If you ask in a very simple and direct way, you use 'can'.

> *<u>Can</u> I ask a question?*
> *<u>Can</u> we have something to wipe our hands on, please?*

'Could' is more polite than 'can'.

> *<u>Could</u> I just interrupt a minute?*
> *<u>Could</u> we put this fire on?*

'May' is also used to ask permission, but this is more formal.

> *<u>May</u> I sit here?*

'Might' is rather old-fashioned and is not often used in modern English in this way.

> _Might_ I inquire if you are the owner?

---

7 You have to use 'be allowed to' instead of a modal if you are using another modal, or if you want to use an '-ing' participle, an '-ed' participle, or a 'to'-infinitive.

> Teachers _will be allowed to_ decide for themselves.
> I am strongly in favour of people _being allowed to_ put on plays.
> They have not _been allowed to_ come.
> We were going _to be allowed to_ travel on the trains.

Unit 93: Instructions and requests

Main points

- You use 'Could you' to tell someone politely to do something.
- Imperatives are not very polite.
- You also use 'Could you' to ask someone politely for help.
- You use 'I would like', 'Would you mind', 'Do you think you could', and 'I wonder if you could' to make requests.

1   When you want to tell someone to do something, you can use 'Could you', 'Will you', and 'Would you'. 'Could you' is very polite.

> _Could you_ make out her bill, please?
> _Could you_ just switch on the light behind you?

'Will you' and 'Would you' are normally used by people in authority. 'Would you' is more polite than 'Will you'.

> _Would you_ tell her that Adrian phoned?
> _Will you_ please leave the room?

Note that although these sentences look like questions ('Will you', not 'You will'), they are not really questions.

2 If someone in authority wants to tell someone to do something, they sometimes say 'I would like you to do this' or 'I'd like you to do this'.

> Penelope, I <u>would like</u> you to get us the files.
> I'<u>d like</u> you to finish this work by Thursday.

3 You can use an imperative to tell someone to do something, but this is not very polite.

> <u>Stop</u> her.
> <u>Go</u> away, all of you.

However, imperatives are commonly used when talking to people you know very well.

> <u>Come</u> here, love.
> <u>Sit down</u> and let me get you a cup of tea.

You often use imperatives in situations of danger or urgency.

> <u>Look out</u>! There's a car coming.
> <u>Put</u> it <u>away</u> before Mum sees you.

4 When you want to ask someone to help you, you use 'Could you', 'Would you', 'Can you', or 'Will you'. 'Could you' and 'Would you' are used in formal situations, or when you want to be very polite, for example because you are asking for something that requires a lot of effort. 'Could you' is more polite than 'Would you'.

> _Could you_ show me how to do this?
> _Would you_ do me a favour?

'Will you' and 'Can you' are used in informal situations, especially when you are not asking for something that requires a lot of effort.

> _Will you_ post this for me on your way to work?
> _Can you_ make me a copy of that?

5 You also use 'I would like' or 'I'd like', followed by a 'to'-infinitive or a noun phrase, to make a request.

> I _would like_ to ask you one question.
> I_'d like_ steak and chips, please.

6 You can also make a request by using:

- 'Would you mind', followed by an '-ing' form

> _Would you mind_ doing the washing up?
> _Would you mind_ waiting a moment?

- 'Do you think you could', followed by the base form of a verb

  Do you think you could help me?

- 'I wonder if you could', followed by the base form of a verb

  I wonder if you could look after my garden for me while I'm away?

Unit 94: Suggestions

Main points

- You use 'could', 'couldn't', or 'shall' to make a suggestion.
- You use 'Shall we' to suggest doing something with someone.
- You use 'You might like' or 'You might want' to make polite suggestions.
- You use 'may as well' or 'might as well' to suggest a sensible action.
- You use 'What about', 'Let's', 'Why don't', and 'Why not' to make suggestions.

1 You use 'could' to suggest doing something.

> You _could_ phone her.
> She _could_ go into research.
> We _could_ go to the cinema on Friday after work.

You also use 'couldn't' in a question to suggest doing something.

> _Couldn't_ you just build some more new factories?
> _Couldn't_ we do it at the weekend?
> _Couldn't_ I sleep on the sofa?

2 You use 'Shall we' to suggest doing something with somebody else.

> *Shall we go and see a film?*
> *Shall we talk about something different now?*

You use 'Shall I' to suggest doing something yourself.

> *Shall I contact the manager?*
> *Shall I go back to the house and get some money?*

---

3 You use 'You might', followed by a verb meaning 'like' or 'want', to make a suggestion in a very polite way.

> *I thought perhaps you might like to come along with me.*
> *You might want to try another shop.*
> *You might prefer to stay in a hotel away from the city centre.*

You can also do this using 'It might be', followed by a noun phrase or an adjective, and a 'to'-infinitive.

> *I think it might be a good idea to stop recording now.*
> *It might be wise to get a new car.*
> *It might be helpful to keep a list of the things you want to do.*

4 You use 'may as well' or 'might as well' to
suggest doing something, but only
because it seems the sensible thing to do,
or because there is no reason not to do it.

> You _may as well_ open them all.
> He _might as well_ take the car.

5 You can also make a suggestion by using:

- 'What about' or 'How about' followed by
  an '-ing' form

  > _What about going_ to Judy's before we go to
  > the party?
  > _How about using_ my car?

- 'Let's' followed by the base form of
  a verb

  > _Let's go_ outside.
  > _Let's talk_ about this after lunch.
  > _Let's start_ as soon as we can.

- 'Why don't I', 'Why don't you' or
  'Why don't we' followed by the base
  form of a verb

  > _Why don't I pick_ you up at seven?
  > _Why don't you write_ to her yourself?
  > _Why don't we just give_ them what they have
  > asked for?

- 'Why not' followed by the base form of a verb

  Why not bring him along?
  Why not try both?
  Why not take some cake home with you?

Unit 95: Offers and invitations

Main points

- You use 'Would you like' to offer something to someone or to invite them to do something.
- You use 'Can I', 'Could I', and 'Shall I' when you offer to help someone.

1 When you are offering something to someone, or inviting them to do something, you use 'Would you like'.

> _Would you like_ a coffee?
> _Would you like_ to come over to my house for a meal?
> _Would you like_ me to take you home?

You can use 'Will you' to offer something to someone you know quite well, or to give an invitation in a fairly informal way.

> _Will you_ have another biscuit, Dave?
> _Will you_ come to my birthday party on Saturday night?

---

2 You use 'Can I' or 'Could I' when you are offering to do something for someone. 'Could I' is more polite.

Can I help you with the dishes?
Could I help you carry those bags?

You also use 'Shall I' when you are offering to do something, especially if you are fairly sure that your offer will be accepted.

Shall I shut the door?
Shall I spell that for you?

3 You use 'I can' or 'I could' to make an offer when you want to say that you are able to help someone.

I have a car. I can take Daisy and Peter to the station.
I could pay some of the rent.

4 You also use 'I'll' to offer to do something.

I'll give them a ring if you like.
I'll show you the hotel.

5 You use 'You must' if you want to invite someone very persuasively to do something.

You must come round for a meal some time next week.
You must come and visit me.

6 There are other ways of making offers and
giving invitations without using modals.
For example, you can use 'Let me' when
offering to help someone.

> _Let me_ take you to your room.
> _Let me_ drive you to London.
> _Let me_ explain why we have taken this
> difficult decision.

You can make an offer or give an invitation
in a more informal way by using an
imperative sentence, when it is clear that
you are not giving an order.

> _Have_ another sandwich.
> _Come_ to my place.
> _Bring_ some friends with you, if you want.

You can add emphasis by putting 'do' in
front of the verb.

> _Do have_ a chocolate biscuit.
> _Do help_ yourselves.
> _Do come in_, Mr Travis.
> _Do tell_ us if there is anything else you need.

You can also give an invitation by using
'Why don't you' or 'How about'.

> _Why don't you_ come to lunch tomorrow?
> _How about_ coming with us to the
> Christmas party?
> _How about_ you come and have dinner with
> me tonight?

Why don't you give me a call when you find it?

Unit 96: Wants and wishes

Main points

- You use 'would like' to say what you want.
- You use 'wouldn't like' to say what you do not want.
- You use 'would rather' or 'would sooner' to say what you prefer.
- You also use 'wouldn't mind' to say what you want.

1 You can say what someone wants by using 'would like' followed by a 'to'-infinitive or a noun phrase.

> I _would like_ to know the date of the next meeting.
> I _would like_ to work in the library.
> John _would like_ his book back.

When the subject is a pronoun, you often use the short form '-'d' instead of 'would'.

> I_'d like_ more information about the work you do.
> We_'d like_ two return tickets to Birmingham, please.

In spoken English, you can also use the short form '-'d' instead of 'would' when the subject is a noun.

> Sally'<u>d like</u> to go to the circus.

---

2 You can say what someone does not want by using 'would not like' or 'wouldn't like'.

> I <u>would not like</u> to see it.
> They <u>wouldn't like</u> that.

---

3 You use 'would like' followed by 'to have' and an '-ed' participle to say that someone wishes now that something had happened in the past, but that it did not happen.

> I <u>would like to have felt</u> more relaxed.
> She'<u>d like to have heard</u> me first.

You use 'would have liked', followed by a 'to'-infinitive or a noun phrase, to say that someone wanted something to happen, but it did not happen.

> Perhaps he <u>would have liked</u> to be a teacher.
> I <u>would have liked</u> more ice cream.

Note the difference. 'Would like to have' refers to present wishes about past events. 'Would have liked' refers to past wishes about past events.

4 You can also use 'would hate', 'would love', or 'would prefer', followed by a 'to'-infinitive or a noun phrase.

> *I <u>would hate</u> to have to move to another house now.*
> *I <u>would love</u> to be able to play the piano like her.*
> *I <u>would prefer</u> a cup of coffee.*

Note that 'would enjoy' is followed by a noun phrase or an '-ing' form, not by a 'to'-infinitive.

> *I <u>would enjoy a bath</u> before we go to the theatre.*
> *I <u>would enjoy seeing</u> him again.*
> *I'<u>d enjoy working</u> with him.*

5 You can use 'would rather' or 'would sooner' followed by the base form of a verb to say that someone prefers one situation to another.

> *I <u>would rather</u> be happy than rich.*
> *He'<u>d rather</u> be playing golf than sitting at his desk.*
> *I'<u>d sooner</u> walk than take the bus.*
> *Most people <u>would sooner</u> borrow money than use their savings.*

6 You use 'I wouldn't mind', followed by an '-ing' form or a noun phrase, to say that you would like to do or have something.

> I _wouldn't mind_ being the manager of
> a store.
> I _wouldn't mind_ a cup of tea.

Unit 97: Obligation and necessity 1

Main points

- You use 'have to', 'must', and 'mustn't' to talk about obligation and necessity in the present and future.

- You use 'had to' to talk about obligation and necessity in the past.

- You use the auxiliary 'do' with 'have to' to make questions.

- You can use 'have got to' in informal English.

1 When you want to say that someone has an obligation to do something, or that it is necessary for them to do it, you use 'must' or 'have to'.

> You <u>must</u> come to the meeting tomorrow.
> The plants <u>must</u> have plenty of sunshine.
> I enjoy parties, unless I <u>have to</u> make a speech.
> He <u>has to</u> travel to find work.

2 There is sometimes a difference between 'must' and 'have to'. When you are stating your own opinion that something is an

obligation or a necessity, you normally use 'must'.

> I *must* be very careful not to upset him.
> We *must* eat before we go.
> He *must* stop working so hard.

When you are giving information about what someone else considers to be an obligation or a necessity, you normally use 'have to'.

> They *have to pay* the bill by Thursday.
> She *has to* go now.

Note that you normally use 'have to' for things that happen repeatedly, especially with adverbs of frequency such as 'often', 'always', and 'regularly'.

> I always *have to* do the shopping.
> You often *have to* wait a long time for a bus.

3 You use 'must not' or 'mustn't' to say that it is important that something is not done or does not happen.

> You *must not* talk about politics.
> They *mustn't* find out that I came here.

Note that 'must not' does not mean the same as 'not have to'. If you 'must not' do something, it is important that you do not do it.

If you 'do not have to' do something, it is not necessary for you to do it, but you can do it if you want.

⚠ BE CAREFUL

You only use 'must' for obligation and necessity in the present and the future. When you want to talk about obligation and necessity in the past, you use 'had to' rather than 'must'.

> She <u>had to</u> catch the six o'clock train.
> I <u>had to</u> wear a suit.

---

4 You use 'do', 'does', or 'did' when you want to make a question using 'have to' and 'not have to'.

> How often <u>do</u> you <u>have to</u> buy petrol for the car?
> <u>Does</u> he <u>have to</u> take so long to get ready?
> What <u>did</u> you <u>have to</u> do?
> <u>Don't</u> you <u>have to</u> be there at one o'clock?

⚠ BE CAREFUL

You do not normally form questions like these by putting a form of 'have' before the subject. For example, you do not normally say 'How often have you to buy petrol?'

5 In informal English, you can use 'have got to' instead of 'have to'.

> You've just got to make sure you tell him.
> She's got to see the doctor.
> Have you got to go so soon?

⚠ BE CAREFUL

You normally use 'had to', not 'had got to', for the past.

> He had to know.
> I had to lend him some money.

---

6 You can only use 'have to', not 'must', if you are using another modal, or if you want to use an '-ing' participle, an '-ed' participle, or a 'to'-infinitive.

> They may have to leave early.
> She grumbled a lot about having to stay abroad.
> I would have had to go through London.
> He doesn't like to have to do the same job every day.

Unit 98: Obligation and necessity 2

Main points

- You use 'need to' to talk about necessity.
- You use 'don't have to', 'don't need to', 'haven't got to', or 'needn't' to say that it is not necessary to do something.
- You use 'needn't' to give someone permission not to do something.
- You use 'need not have', 'needn't have', 'didn't need to', or 'didn't have to' to say that it was not necessary to do something in the past.

1 You can use 'need to' to talk about the necessity of doing something.

You might <u>need to</u> see a doctor.
A number of questions <u>need to</u> be asked.

2 You use 'don't have to' when there is no obligation or necessity to do something.

You <u>don't have to</u> learn any new typing skills for the job.
Rebecca is lucky - she <u>doesn't have to</u> work.

You can also use 'don't need to', 'haven't got to', or 'needn't' to say that there is no obligation or necessity to do something.

> *You <u>don't need to</u> buy anything.*
> *I <u>haven't got to</u> go to work today.*
> *I can pick John up later on tonight. You <u>needn't</u> bother.*

---

3 You also use 'needn't' when you are giving someone permission not to do something.

> *You <u>needn't</u> say anything if you really don't want to.*
> *You <u>needn't</u> stay any longer tonight.*
> *We <u>needn't</u> go to the party if you don't want to.*

---

4 You use 'need not have' or 'needn't have' and an '-ed' participle to say that someone did something which was not necessary. You are often implying that the person did not know at the time that their action was not necessary.

> *He <u>need not have</u> bothered to return early.*
> *It turned out that we <u>need not have</u> hurried back.*
> *The boys <u>needn't have</u> waited until the game began.*
> *We <u>needn't have</u> worried about our lack of experience.*

---

5 You use 'didn't need to' to say that something was not necessary, and that it was known at the time that the action was not necessary. You do not know if the action was done, unless you are given more information.

> I _didn't need_ to worry.
> They _didn't need_ to talk about it, he already knew.

---

6 You also use 'didn't have to' to say that it was not necessary to do something.

> He _didn't have to_ speak.
> As a matter of fact, Bill and I _didn't have to_ pay.

---

7 You cannot use 'must' to refer to the past, so when you want to say that it was important that something did not happen or was not done, you use other expressions.

You can say 'It was important not to', or use phrases like 'had to make sure' or 'had to make certain' in a negative sentence.

> It was _important_ not to take the game too seriously.
> It was _necessary_ that no one was aware of being watched.

You <u>had to make sure</u> that you didn't
spend too much.
We <u>had to</u> do our best to <u>make certain</u> that
it wasn't out of date.

Unit 99: Mild obligation and advice

Main points

- You use 'should' and 'ought' to talk about mild obligation.
- You use 'should have' and 'ought to have' to say that there was a mild obligation to do something in the past, but it was not done.
- You can also use 'had better' to talk about mild obligation.

1 You can use 'should' and 'ought' to talk about a mild obligation to do something. When you use 'should' and 'ought', you are saying that the feeling of obligation is not as strong as when you use 'must'.

'Should' and 'ought' are very common in spoken English.

'Should' is followed by the base form of a verb, but 'ought' is followed by a 'to'-infinitive.

When you want to say that there is a mild obligation not to do something, you use 'should not', 'shouldn't, 'ought not', or 'oughtn't'.

2 You use 'should' and 'ought' in three main ways:

- when you are talking about what is a good thing to do, or the right thing to do.

  We <u>should</u> send her a postcard.
  We <u>shouldn't</u> spend all the money.
  He <u>ought</u> to come more often.
  You <u>ought not</u> to see him again.

- when you are trying to advise someone about what to do or what not to do.

  You <u>should</u> claim your pension 3-4 months before you retire.
  You <u>shouldn't</u> use a detergent.
  You <u>ought</u> to get a new TV.
  You <u>oughtn't</u> to marry him.

- when you are giving or asking for an opinion about a situation. You often use 'I think', 'I don't think', or 'Do you think' to start the sentence.

  I think that we <u>should</u> be paid more.
  I don't think we <u>ought</u> to grumble.
  Do you think he <u>ought not</u> to go?
  What do you think we <u>should</u> do?

3 You use 'should have' or 'ought to have' and an '-ed' participle to say that there was a mild obligation to do something in the past, but that it was not done.

For example, if you say 'I should have given him the money yesterday', you mean that you had a mild obligation to give him the money yesterday, but you did not give it to him.

> I _should have_ gone straight home.
> You _should have_ realised that he was only joking.
> We _ought to have_ stayed in tonight.
> They _ought to have_ taken a taxi.

You use 'should not have' or 'ought not to have' and an '-ed' participle to say that it was important not to do something in the past, but that it was done. For example, if you say 'I should not have left the door open', you mean that it was important that you did not leave the door open, but you did leave it open.

> I _should not have_ said that.
> You _shouldn't have_ given him the money.
> They _ought not to have_ told him.
> She _oughtn't to have_ sold the ring.

---

4 You use 'had better' followed by a base form to indicate mild obligation to do something in a particular situation. You also use 'had better' when giving advice or when giving your opinion about something. The negative is 'had better not'.

I think I <u>had better</u> show this to you now.
You'<u>d better</u> go tomorrow.
I'<u>d better not</u> look at this.

⚠ BE CAREFUL

The correct form is always 'had better'
(not 'have better'). You do not use 'had
better' to talk about mild obligation in
the past, even though it looks like a
past form.

Unit 100: Defining relative clauses

Main points

- You use defining relative clauses to say exactly which person or thing you are talking about.
- Defining relative clauses are usually introduced by a relative pronoun such as 'that', 'which', 'who', 'whom', or 'whose'.
- A defining relative clause comes immediately after a noun, and needs a main clause to make a complete sentence.

1 You use defining relative clauses to give information that helps to identify the person or thing you are talking about.

> *The man <u>who you met yesterday</u> was my brother.*
> *The car <u>which crashed into me</u> belonged to Paul.*

When you are talking about people, you use 'that' or 'who' in the relative clause.

> *He was the man <u>that</u> bought my house.*
> *You are the only person here <u>who</u> knows me.*

When you are talking about things, you use 'that' or 'which' in the relative clause.

There was ice cream <u>that</u> Mum had made herself.

I'll tell you the first thing <u>which</u> I can remember.

2 'That', 'who', or 'which' can be:

- the subject of the verb in the relative clause

  The thing <u>that</u> surprised me was his attitude.

  The woman <u>who</u> lives next door is very friendly.

  The car <u>which</u> caused the accident drove off.

- the object of the verb in the relative clause

  The thing <u>that</u> I really liked about it was its size.

  The woman <u>who</u> you met yesterday lives next door.

  The car <u>which</u> I wanted to buy was not for sale.

In formal English, 'whom' is used instead of 'who' as the object of the verb in the relative clause.

She was a woman <u>whom</u> I greatly respected.

3 You can leave out 'that', 'who', or 'which' when they are the object of the verb in the relative clause.

> *The woman you met yesterday lives next door.*
> *The car I wanted to buy was not for sale.*
> *The thing I really liked about it was its size.*

⚠ BE CAREFUL

You cannot leave out 'that', 'who', or 'which' when they are the subject of the verb in the relative clause. For example, you say 'The woman who lives next door is very friendly'. You do not say 'The woman lives next door is very friendly'.

---

4 A relative pronoun in a relative clause can be the object of a preposition. Usually the preposition goes at the end of the clause.

> *I wanted to do the job <u>which</u> I'd been training <u>for</u>.*
> *The house <u>that</u> we lived <u>in</u> was huge.*

You can often omit a relative pronoun that is the object of a preposition.

> *Angela was the only person <u>I could talk to</u>.*
> *She's the girl <u>I sang the song for</u>.*

The preposition always goes in front of 'whom', and in front of 'which' in formal English.

These are the people <u>to whom</u> Catherine was referring.
He was asking questions <u>to which</u> there were no answers.

---

5 You use 'whose' in relative clauses to indicate who something belongs to or relates to. You normally use 'whose' for people, not for things.

A child <u>whose</u> mother had left him was crying loudly.
We have only told the people <u>whose</u> work is relevant to this project.

---

6 You can use 'when', 'where', and 'why' in defining relative clauses after certain nouns. You use 'when' after 'time' or time words such as 'day' or 'year'. You use 'where' after 'place' or place words such as 'room' or 'street'. You use 'why' after 'reason'.

There had been <u>a time when</u> she hated all men.
This is <u>the year when</u> profits should increase.
He showed me <u>the place where</u> they work.
That was <u>the room where</u> I did my homework.
There are several <u>reasons why</u> we can't do that.

Unit 101: Non-defining relative clauses

Main points

- You use non-defining relative clauses to give extra information about the person or thing you are talking about.

- Non-defining relative clauses must be introduced by a relative pronoun such as 'which', 'who', 'whom', or 'whose'.

- A non-defining relative clause comes immediately after a noun and needs a main clause to make a complete sentence.

1 You use non-defining relative clauses to give extra information about the person or thing you are talking about. The information is not needed to identify that person or thing.

> *Professor Marvin, <u>who was always early</u>, was there already.*

'Who was always early' gives extra information about Professor Marvin. This is a non-defining relative clause, because it is not needed to identify the person you are talking about. We already know that you are talking about Professor Marvin.

Note that in written English, a non-defining relative clause is usually separated from the main clause by a comma, or by two commas.

> *I went to the cinema with Mary, who you met.*
> *British Rail, which has launched an enquiry, said one coach was badly damaged.*

2 You always start a non-defining relative clause with a relative pronoun. When you are talking about people, you use 'who'. 'Who' can be the subject or object of a non-defining relative clause.

> *Heath Robinson, <u>who</u> died in 1944, was a graphic artist and cartoonist.*
> *I was in the same group as Janice, <u>who</u> I like a lot.*

In formal English, 'whom' is sometimes used instead of 'who' as the object of a non-defining relative clause.

> *She was engaged to a sailor, <u>whom</u> she had met at Dartmouth.*

3 When you are talking about things, you use 'which' as the subject or object of a non-defining relative clause.

> I am teaching at the local college, <u>which</u>
> is just over the road.
> He had a lot of money, <u>which</u> he spent
> mainly on cars.

⚠ **BE CAREFUL**

You do not normally use 'that' in non-defining relative clauses.

4 You can also use a non-defining relative clause beginning with 'which' to say something about the whole situation described in a main clause.

> I never met Brendan again, <u>which</u> was
> a pity.
> She was a little tense, <u>which</u> was
> understandable.
> Small computers need only small amounts
> of power, <u>which</u> means that they will run
> on small batteries.

5 When you are talking about a group of people or things and then want to say something about only some of them, you can use one of the following expressions:

many of which	many of whom
none of which	none of whom
one of which	one of whom
some of which	some of whom

> *They were all friends, <u>many of whom</u> had*
> *known each other for years.*
> *He talked about several very interesting*
> *people, <u>some of whom</u> he was still in*
> *contact with.*

---

6 You can use 'when' and 'where' in
   non-defining relative clauses after
   expressions of time or place.

> *This happened in 1957, <u>when</u> I was still*
> *a baby.*
> *She has just come back from a holiday in*
> *Crete, <u>where</u> Alex and I went last year.*

Unit 102:
Participle clauses

Main points

- Nouns are followed by '-ing' clauses that say what a person or thing is doing.
- Nouns are followed by '-ed' clauses that show that a person or thing has been affected or caused by an action.

1 You can often give more information about a noun, or an indefinite pronoun such as 'someone' or 'something', by adding a clause beginning with an '-ing' participle, an '-ed' participle, or a 'to'-infinitive.

> He gestured towards <u>the box lying on the table</u>.
> I think <u>the idea suggested by Tim</u> is the best one.
> She wanted <u>someone to talk to</u>.

2 You use an '-ing' clause after a noun to say what someone or something is doing or was doing at a particular time.

> The young girl <u>sitting opposite him</u> was his daughter.
> Most of the people <u>strolling in the park</u> were teenagers.

3 You can also use an '-ing' clause after a noun to say what a person or thing does generally, rather than at a particular time.

> Problems _facing parents_ should be discussed.
> The men _working there_ were not very friendly.

4 You often use an '-ing' clause after a noun which is the object of a verb of perception, such as 'see', 'hear', or 'feel'.
→ See also Unit 80.

> Suddenly we saw Amy _walking down the path_.
> He heard a distant voice _shouting_.
> I could feel something _touching my face and neck_, something ice-cold.

5 You use an '-ed' clause after a noun to show that someone or something has been affected or caused by an action.

> He was the new minister _appointed by the President_.
> The man _injured in the accident_ was taken to hospital.

Remember that not all verbs have regular '-ed' participles.

> A story _written by a young girl_ won the competition.
> She was wearing a dress _bought in Paris_.

Unit 103: Adding to a noun phrase

Main points

- Some adjectives can be used after nouns.
- You can use relative clauses after nouns.
- Adverbials of place and time can come after nouns.
- A noun can be followed by another noun phrase.
- You can use 'that'-clauses after some nouns.

1 You can use some adjectives after a noun to give more information about it, but the adjectives are usually followed by a prepositional phrase, a 'to'-infinitive clause, or an adverbial.

> This is a warning to people _eager for a quick profit_.
> These are the weapons _likely to be used_.
> For a list of the facilities _available here_, ask the secretary.
> You must talk to the people _concerned_.

→ See Unit 36 for more information on adjectives used after nouns.

2 When you want to give more precise information about the person or thing you are talking about, you can use a defining relative clause after the noun.

> *The man <u>who had done it</u> was arrested.*
> *There are a lot of things <u>that are wrong</u>.*
> *Nearly all the people <u>I used to know</u> have gone.*

Note that you can also use defining relative clauses after indefinite pronouns such as 'someone' or 'something'.

> *I'm talking about somebody <u>who is really ill</u>.*

→ See Unit 100 for more information on defining relative clauses.

3 You can use an adverbial of place or time after a noun.

> *People <u>everywhere</u> are becoming more selfish.*
> *This is a reflection of life <u>today</u>.*

4 You can add a second noun phrase after a noun. The second noun phrase gives you more precise information about the first noun.

> *Her mother, <u>a Canadian</u>, died when she was six.*

Note that the second noun phrase is separated by commas from the rest of the clause.

5 Nouns such as 'advice', 'hope', and 'wish', which refer to what someone says or thinks, can be followed by a 'that'-clause. Here are some examples:

advice	agreement	belief	claim
conclusion	decision	feeling	hope
promise	threat	warning	wish

It is my firm <u>belief that</u> different children need different types of school.
I had a <u>feeling that</u> no-one thought I was good enough.

Note that all these nouns are related to reporting verbs, which also take a 'that'-clause. For example, 'information' is related to 'inform', and 'decision' is related to 'decide'.

Some of these nouns can also be followed by a 'to'-infinitive clause.

agreement	decision	hope	order
promise	threat	warning	wish

The <u>decision to go</u> had not been an easy one.
I reminded Jim of his <u>promise to take us all out for lunch</u>.

6 A few other nouns can be followed by
   a 'that'-clause.

advantage	confidence	danger
effect	evidence	fact
idea	impression	news
opinion	possibility	view

> *He didn't want her to get the <u>idea that</u>
> he was rich.*
> *I had no <u>evidence that</u> Jed was the killer.*
> *He couldn't believe the <u>news that</u> his house
> had just burned down.*

Note that when a noun phrase is the
object of a verb, it may be followed by
different structures.

Unit 104: Time clauses

Main points

- You use time clauses to say when something happens.
- Time clauses can refer to the past, present, or future.
- Time clauses are introduced by words such as 'after', 'when', or 'while'.
- A time clause needs a main clause to make a complete sentence. The time clause can come before or after the main clause.

1 You use time clauses to say when something happens. The verb in the time clause can be in a present or a past tense form.

> I look after the children <u>while</u> she <u>goes</u> to London.
> I haven't given him a thing to eat <u>since</u> he <u>arrived</u>.

⚠ BE CAREFUL

You never use a future form in a time clause. You use one of the present tense forms instead.

> *Let me stay here <u>till</u> Jeannie <u>comes</u> to bed.*
> *I'll do it <u>when</u> I'<u>ve finished</u> writing this letter.*

---

2 When you want to say that two events happen at the same time, you use a time clause with 'as', 'when', or 'while'.

> *We arrived <u>as they were leaving</u>.*

Sometimes the two events happen together for a period of time.

> *She cried <u>as she told her story</u>.*

Sometimes one event interrupts another event.

> *He was having his dinner <u>when</u> the telephone rang.*
> *John will arrive <u>while</u> we are watching the film.*

Note that you often use a progressive form for the interrupted action.
→ See Unit 68.

---

3 When you want to say that one event happens before or after another event, you use a time clause with 'after', 'as soon as', 'before', or 'when'.

> <u>*As soon as*</u> *we get tickets, we'll send them to you.*
> *Can I see you <u>before</u> you go, Helen?*
> <u>*When*</u> *he had finished reading, he looked up.*

Note that you use the past perfect to indicate an event that happened before another event in the past.

---

4 When you want to mention a situation which started in the past and continued until a later time, you use a time clause with 'since' or 'ever since'. You use the past simple or past perfect in the time clause, and the past perfect in the main clause.

He hadn't cried <u>since he was</u> a boy of ten.
Janine had been busy <u>ever since she had heard</u> the news.
I<u>'d wanted</u> to come ever since I was a child.

If the situation started in the past and still continues now, you use the past simple in the time clause, and the present perfect in the main clause.

I've been in politics <u>since I was</u> at university.
Ever since you arrived <u>you've been causing</u> trouble.

Note that after impersonal 'it' and a time expression, if the main clause is in the present tense, you use 'since' with the past simple.

It <u>is</u> two weeks now since I <u>wrote</u> to you.

If the main clause is in the past tense, you use 'since' with the past perfect.

It <u>was</u> nearly seven years since I<u>'d seen</u> Toby.

→ For 'since' as a preposition, see Unit 48.

5 When you want to talk about when a situation ends, you use a time clause with 'till' or 'until' and a present or past tense form.

> We'll support them _till they find_ work.
> I stayed there talking to them _until I saw_ Sam.
> She waited _until he had gone_.

6 When you want to say that something happens before or at a particular time, you use a time clause with 'by the time' or 'by which time'.

> _By the time_ I went to bed, I was exhausted.
> He came back later, _by which time_ they _had gone_.

7 In written or formal English, if the subject of the main clause and the time clause are the same, you sometimes omit the subject in the time clause and use a participle as the verb.

> I read the book _before going_ to see the film.
> The car was stolen _while parked_ in a London street.

Unit 105: Purpose and reason clauses

Main points

- Purpose clauses are introduced by conjunctions such as 'so', 'so as to', 'so that', 'in order to', or 'in order that'.
- Reason clauses are introduced by conjunctions such as 'as', 'because', or 'in case'.
- A purpose or reason clause needs a main clause to make a complete sentence.
- A purpose clause usually comes after a main clause. A reason clause can come before or after a main clause.

1 You use a purpose clause when you are saying what someone's intention is when they do something. The most common type of purpose clause is a 'to'-infinitive clause.

> *The children sleep together <u>to keep</u> warm.*
> *They locked the door <u>to stop</u> us from getting in.*

Instead of using an ordinary 'to'-infinitive, you often use 'in order to' or 'so as to' with an infinitive.

> *He gave up his job <u>in order to stay</u> at home.*
> *I keep the window open, <u>so as to let</u> fresh air in.*

To make a purpose clause negative, you have to use 'in order not to' or 'so as not to' with an infinitive.

> *I would have to give myself something to do <u>in order not to</u> be bored.*
> *They went on foot, <u>so as not to</u> be heard.*

Another way of making purpose clauses negative is by using 'to avoid' with an '-ing' form or a noun phrase.

> *I had to turn away <u>to avoid letting</u> him see my smile.*
> *They drove through town <u>to avoid the motorway</u>.*

2 Another type of purpose clause begins with 'in order that', 'so', or 'so that'. These clauses usually contain a modal.

When the main clause refers to the present, you usually use 'can', 'may', 'will', or 'shall' in the purpose clause.

> *Any holes should be fenced <u>so that</u> people <u>can't</u> fall down them.*

> *I have drawn a diagram <u>so that</u> my explanation <u>will</u> be clearer.*

When the main clause refers to the past, you usually use 'could', 'might', 'should', or 'would' in the purpose clause.

> *She said she wanted dinner ready at six <u>so</u> she <u>could</u> be out by eight.*
> *Someone lifted Philip onto his shoulder <u>so that</u> he <u>might</u> see the procession.*

You use 'in order that', 'so', and 'so that', when the subject of the purpose clause is different from the subject of the main clause. For example, you say 'I've underlined it so that it will be easier.' You do not say 'I've underlined it to be easier'.

---

3 You can also talk about the purpose of an action by using a prepositional phrase introduced by 'for'.

> *She went out <u>for a run</u>.*
> *They said they did it <u>for fun</u>.*
> *I usually check, just <u>for safety's sake</u>.*

---

4 You use a reason clause when you want to explain why someone does something or why it happens. When you are simply giving the reason for something, you use 'because', 'since', or 'as'.

*I couldn't see Helen's expression, because
her head was turned.*
Since it was Saturday, he stayed in bed.
*As he had been up since 4 am, he was
very tired.*

You can also use 'why' and a reported
question to talk about the reason for
an action.
→ See Unit 83.

I asked him why he had come.

5 When you are talking about a possible
situation which explains the reason why
someone does something, you use 'in
case' or 'just in case'.

I've got the key in case we want to go inside.
*I am here just in case anything unusual
happens.*

⚠ **BE CAREFUL**

You do not use a future form after 'in case'.
You do not say 'I'll stay behind in case she'll
arrive later'.

Unit 106: Result clauses

Main points

- You use result clauses to talk about the result of an action or situation.

- Result clauses are introduced by conjunctions such as 'so', 'so...(that)', or 'such...(that)'.

- A result clause needs a main clause to make a complete sentence. The result clause always comes after the main clause.

1 You use 'so' and 'so that' to say what the result of an action or situation is.

> He speaks very little English, _so_ I talked to him through an interpreter.
> My suitcase had become damaged on the journey home, _so that_ the lid would not stay closed.

2 You also use 'so...that' or 'such...that' to talk about the result of an action or situation.

> He dressed _so_ quickly _that_ he put his boots on the wrong feet.

She got <u>such</u> a shock <u>that</u> she dropped the bag.

'That' is often omitted.

They were <u>so</u> surprised they didn't try to stop him.
They got <u>such</u> a fright they ran away.

---

3   You only use 'such' before a noun, with or without an adjective.

They obeyed him with <u>such willingness</u> that the strike went on for over a year.
Sometimes they say <u>such stupid things</u> that I don't even bother to listen.

If the noun is a singular countable noun, you put 'a' or 'an' in front of it.

I was in <u>such a panic</u> that I didn't know it was him.

Note that you only use 'so' before an adjective or an adverb.

It all sounded <u>so crazy</u> that I laughed out loud.
They worked <u>so quickly</u> that there was no time for talking.

---

4   When you want to say that a situation does not happen because someone or something has an excessive amount of a quality, you use 'too' with an adjective

and a 'to'-infinitive. For example, if you say 'They were too tired to walk', you mean that they did not walk because they were too tired.

> *He was <u>too proud to apologise</u>.*
> *She was <u>too weak to lift</u> me.*

You also use 'too' with an adverb and a 'to'-infinitive.

> *They had been walking <u>too silently to be heard</u>.*
> *She spoke <u>too quickly</u> for me <u>to understand</u>.*

---

5 When you want to say that a situation happens or is possible because someone or something has a sufficient amount of a quality, you use 'enough' after adjectives and adverbs, followed by a 'to'-infinitive.

> *He was <u>old enough to understand</u>.*
> *I could see <u>well enough to know</u> we were losing.*

You normally put 'enough' in front of a noun, not after it.

> *I don't think I've got <u>enough information to speak</u> confidently.*

---

6 You also use 'and as a result', 'and so', or 'and therefore' to talk about the result of an action or situation.

> He had been ill for six months, _and as_
> _a result_ had lost his job.
> She was having difficulty getting her car out,
> _and so_ I had to move my car to let her out.
> We have a growing population _and therefore_
> we need more and more food.

You can also put 'therefore' after the
subject of the clause. For example, you
can say 'We have a growing population
and we therefore need more food'.

'As a result' and 'therefore' can also be used
at the beginning of a separate sentence.

> In a group, patients are not so frightened.
> _As a result_, they talk about their problems
> more easily.
> He lacks money to invest in improving his
> tools. _Therefore_ he is poor.

Unit 107: Contrast clauses

Main points

- These are clauses introduced by 'although', 'in spite of' and 'though'.
- You use contrast clauses when you want to make two statements, and one statement makes the other seem surprising.
- Contrast clauses are introduced by conjunctions such as 'although', 'in spite of', or 'though'.
- A contrast clause needs a main clause to make a complete sentence. The contrast clause can come before or after the main clause.

1 When you simply want to contrast two statements, you use 'although', 'though' or 'even though'.

> <u>Although</u> he was late, he stopped to buy a sandwich.
> <u>Though</u> he has lived for years in London, he writes in German.
> I used to love listening to her, <u>even though</u> I could only understand about half of what she said.

Sometimes you use words like 'still', 'nevertheless', or 'just the same' in the main clause to add emphasis to the contrast.

Although I was shocked, I *still* couldn't blame him.
Although his company is profitable, it *nevertheless* needs to face up to some serious problems.
Although she hated them, she agreed to help them *just the same*.

When the subject of the contrast clause and the main clause are the same, you can often omit the subject and the verb 'be' in the contrast clause.

Although poor, we still have our pride. (Although we are poor...)
Though dying of cancer, he painted every day. (Though he was dying of cancer...)

2 Another way of making a contrast is to use 'despite' or 'in spite of', followed by a noun phrase.

Despite the difference in their ages they were close friends.
In spite of poor health, my father was always cheerful.

⚠️ **BE CAREFUL**

You say 'in spite of' but 'despite' without 'of'.

> His mind was still extremely active, _in spite of_ his age.
> Henry is very healthy, _despite_ his age.

---

3   You can also use an '-ing' participle after 'despite' or 'in spite of'.

> _Despite working_ hard, I failed all my university exams.
> The club was relegated _despite winning_ its last match.
> We had higher profits _in spite of paying_ higher wages than the previous owner.

4   You can also use 'despite the fact that' or 'in spite of the fact that', followed by a clause.

> _Despite the fact that_ it sounds like science fiction, most of it is technically possible at this moment.
> They ignored this order, _in spite of the fact that_ they would probably get into a great deal of trouble.

It is possible to omit 'that', especially in spoken English.

He insisted on playing, <u>in spite of the fact he had a bad cold</u>.
<u>*Despite the fact they live in the same city,*</u>
they lead very different lives.

Unit 108: Manner clauses

Main points

- You use manner clauses to talk about how something is done.
- Manner clauses are introduced by conjunctions such as 'as', 'as if', 'as though', or 'like'.
- A manner clause needs a main clause to make a complete sentence. The manner clause always comes after the main clause.

1 When you want to say how someone does something, or how something is done, you use 'as'.

> He behaves _as_ he does, because his father was really cruel to him.
> The bricks are made _as_ they were in Roman times.
> I live _as_ I always intended to live.

You often use 'just', 'exactly', or 'precisely' in front of 'as' for emphasis.

> It swims on the sea floor _just as_ its ancestors did.
> I attended a boarding school, _just as_ my father had done.

He reacted to the news <u>exactly as</u> she wanted him to.
I like to plan my day <u>exactly as</u> I want.
Everything went <u>precisely as</u> she had planned.
The eggs were produced <u>precisely as</u> they were in his childhood.

2   When you want to indicate that the information in the manner clause might not be true, or is definitely not true, you use 'as if' or 'as though'.

Almost <u>as if</u> she'd read his thought, she returned to her seat.
She reacted <u>as if</u> she had been punched in the stomach.
He behaved <u>as though</u> he had only just begun the investigation.
Just act <u>as though</u> everything's normal.

After 'as if' or 'as though', you often use a past tense form even when you are talking about the present, to emphasize that the information in the manner clause is not true. In formal English, you use 'were' instead of 'was'.

She treats him <u>as if</u> he <u>had</u> some sort of illness.
He often behaves <u>as though</u> I <u>wasn't</u> there.

*The Amercians are acting <u>as though</u> the
quarrel <u>were</u> a minor nuisance.*

→ See also Unit 76.

---

3 You also use 'the way (that)', 'in a way
(that)', or 'in the way (that)' to talk about
how someone does something, or how
something is done.

*I was never allowed to sing <u>the way</u> I
wanted to.*
*They did it <u>in a way that</u> I had never seen
before.*
*We make it move <u>in the way that</u> we want
it to.*

---

4 You can use 'how' in questions and
reported questions to talk about the
method used to do something, and
sometimes to indicate your surprise that
it was possible to do it.

*'<u>How</u> did he get in to the flat?' – 'He broke
a window.'*
I wondered <u>how</u> he could afford a new car.
*<u>How</u> did they manage to get the goods
across the border?*
*I don't know <u>how</u> she was able to joke at
such a difficult time.*

Sometimes, you can use 'how' to talk about the manner in which someone does something.

> I watched <u>how</u> he did it, then tried to copy him.
> Tell me <u>how</u> he reacted when he finally saw you.
> Listen to <u>how</u> she talks to Harry on the telephone.
> I was encouraged by <u>how</u> we played on Saturday.

Unit 109: Changing sentence focus

Main points

- You can sometimes change the focus of a sentence by moving part of the sentence to the front.

- You can also change the focus of a sentence by using an expression such as 'The fact is', 'The thing is', or 'The problem is'.

- You can also use impersonal 'it' to change the focus of a sentence.

1 In most affirmative clauses, the subject of the verb comes first.

> _They_ went to Australia in 1956.
> _I_'ve no idea who it was.

However, when you want to emphasize another part of the sentence, you can put that part first instead.

> _In 1956_ they went to Australia.
> _Who it was_ I've no idea.

2 One common way of giving emphasis is by placing an adverbial at the beginning of the sentence.

> <u>At eight o'clock</u> I went downstairs for my breakfast.
> <u>For years</u> I'd had to hide what I was thinking.

Note that after adverbials of place and negative adverbials, you normally put the subject after the verb.

> She rang the bell for Sylvia. In <u>came a girl</u> she had not seen before.
> On no account <u>must they</u> be let in.

After adverbials of place, you can also put the subject before the verb. You must do so, if the subject is a pronoun.

> The door opened and <u>in she came</u>.
> He'd chosen Japan, so <u>off we went</u> to the Japanese Embassy.

3 When you want to say that you do not know something, you can put a reported question at the beginning of the sentence.

> <u>What I'm going to do next</u> I don't quite know.
> <u>How he managed</u> I can't imagine.

4 Another way of focusing on information is to use a structure which introduces what you want to say by using 'the' and a noun, followed by 'is'.

The nouns most commonly used in this way are:

answer	conclusion	fact	point
problem	question	rule	solution
thing	trouble	truth	

The second part of the sentence is usually a 'that'-clause or a 'wh'-clause, although it can also be a 'to'-infinitive clause or a noun phrase.

> _The problem is_ that she can't cook.
> _The thing is,_ how are we going to get her out?
> _The solution is_ to adopt the policy which will produce the greatest benefits.
> _The answer is_ planning, timing, and, above all, practical experience.

It is also common to use a whole sentence to introduce information in following sentences.

→ See Unit 110 for more information.

5 You can also focus on information by using impersonal 'it', followed by 'be', a noun phrase, and a relative clause.

The noun phrase can be the subject or object of the relative clause.

> _It was Ted who_ broke the news to me.

It is usually *the other vehicle that*
suffers most.
It's money that they want.
It was me Daniel wanted.

There are many other ways of focusing
on information:

Ted was the one who broke the news to me.
Money is what we want.
What we want is money.

---

6 You can also focus on the information
given in the other parts of a clause, or
a whole clause, using impersonal 'it'.
In this case, the second part of the
sentence is a 'that'-clause.

It was from Francis that she first heard
the news.
It was meeting Peter that really started
me off on this new line of work.
Perhaps it's because he's different that
I get along with him.

Unit 110: Cohesion

Main points

- You can use pronouns and determiners to refer back to something that has already been mentioned.
- You use coordinating conjunctions to link clauses.

1 When you speak or write, you usually need to make some connection with other things that you are saying or writing. The most common way of doing this is by referring back to something that has already been mentioned.

2 One way of referring back to something is to use a personal pronoun such as 'she', 'it', or 'them', or a possessive pronoun such as 'mine' or 'hers'.

> _My father_ is American. _He_ was born in New Jersey.
> _Mary_ came in. _She_ was a good-looking woman.
> 'Have you been to _London_?' – 'Yes, _it_ was very crowded.'
> 'Have you heard of _David Lodge_?' – 'Yes, I've just read a novel of _his_.'
> 'Would you mind moving _your car_, please?' – 'It's not _mine_.'

3 You can also use a specific determiner such as 'the' or 'his' in front of a noun to refer back to something.

> A <u>man</u> and a <u>woman</u> were walking up the hill. <u>The</u> man wore shorts and a T-shirt. <u>The</u> woman wore a long dress.
> 'Thanks,' said Brody. He put the telephone down, turned out the light in <u>his</u> office, and walked out to <u>his</u> car.

4 The demonstratives 'this', 'that', 'these' and 'those' are also used to refer back to a thing or fact that has just been mentioned.

> In 1973 he went on a <u>caravan holiday</u>. At the beginning of <u>this</u> holiday he began to experience pain in his chest.
> There's a lot of <u>material</u> there. You can use some of <u>that</u>.

5 The following general determiners can also be used to refer back to something:

another	both	each	either
every	neither	other	

> Five <u>officials</u> were sacked. <u>Another</u> four were arrested.
> There are more than two hundred and fifty <u>species of shark</u>, and <u>every</u> one is different.

6 Another common way of making connections in spoken or written English is by using one of the following coordinating conjunctions:

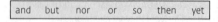

| and | but | nor | or | so | then | yet |

Anna had to go into town <u>and</u> she wanted to go to Bride Street.
I asked if I could borrow her bicycle <u>but</u> she refused.
He was only a boy then, <u>yet</u> he was not afraid.

You can use a coordinating conjunction to link clauses that have the same subject. When you link clauses which have the same subject, you do not always need to repeat the subject in the second clause.

She was born in Budapest <u>and</u> raised in Manhattan.
He didn't yell <u>or</u> scream.
When she saw Morris she went pale, <u>then</u> blushed.

7 Most subordinating conjunctions can also be used to link sentences together, rather than to link a subordinate clause with a main clause in the same sentence.

'When will you do it?' – '<u>When</u> I get time.'

'Can I borrow your car?' – '<u>So long as</u> you
drive carefully.'
We send that by airmail. <u>Therefore</u>, it's away
on Thursday and our client gets it on
Monday.

---

8 When people are speaking or writing, they
often use words that refer back to similar
words, or words that refer back to a
whole sentence or paragraph.

Everything was <u>quiet</u>. Everywhere there
was the <u>silence</u> of the winter night.
'<u>What are you going to do?</u>' – 'That's a good
<u>question</u>.'

The grammar of academic English

Introduction

When people write or speak in academic contexts (for example in lectures, presentations, essays, journal articles, or academic books), they use certain common grammatical patterns. This unit describes the following aspects of academic English:

- focusing on nouns
- talking about states and processes
- reporting the work of other academics
- connecting your message
- academic style.

Focusing on nouns

Academic English focuses more on concepts and ideas than on events and actions. Therefore, verbs are often nominalized (= made into nouns). For example:

verb	noun
demonstrate	demonstration
discover	discovery
measure	measurement
assess	assessment
assist	assistance
maintain	maintenance

In 1898 Marie and Pierre Curie announced their <u>discovery</u> *of a new element.*
Laboratory technicians can provide <u>assistance</u> *when required.*

Because academic English focuses more on nouns, noun phrases are often longer. You can put more information into the noun phrase by using adjectives or other nouns as modifiers.

> *...a* <u>food preservation process</u>.
> *...the results of a* <u>three-year scientific research project</u>.

Talking about states and processes

The range of verb forms used in academic English is more restricted than in everyday English. Simple forms of verbs are used more frequently. Progressive forms, the past perfect, and the future perfect are used less often.

The present simple is mainly used to refer to general principles or laws, and to situations that are still true.

> *When water* <u>freezes</u>, *it* <u>expands</u>.
> *This theory* <u>is</u> *based on two main concepts:...*

The present simple is also used to describe results, and to refer to the work of other academics.

> *The results* <u>show</u> *that only a portion of world trade is affected.*

> *Gaudet (2009) <u>discusses</u> these trends in detail.*

The present perfect is mainly used to describe the state of research on a particular subject, or to summarize a text.

> *Little research <u>has been carried out</u> on microscopic plastics.*
> *This section <u>has described</u> current methods of data collection.*

The past simple is mainly used to describe procedures, and to report findings.

> *Participants <u>were</u> selected from a random sample of schools.*
> *Their research <u>showed</u> that over half of all cancer cases could be prevented.*

Reporting the work of other academics

An important aspect of academic speaking and writing is reporting the work of other academics. The following are some common reporting verbs used in academic English.

argue	establish	show
believe	estimate	state
calculate	explain	suggest
claim	find	write
conclude	focus on	
demonstrate	imply	
discuss	maintain	

*Wenger's data <u>show</u> that obesity is
becoming more common in all age groups.
Smith (1998) <u>argues</u> that the most
important factors are as follows:...
Collins and Ellis (2010) <u>focus on</u> problems in
early childhood.*

Connecting your message

It is important to organize academic texts in
a logical and coherent way. This section
describes grammatical structures you can
use to connect your message.

Referring back and referring forward

'This' can be used to refer back to ideas,
events, and other pieces of writing.

*<u>This view</u> is also held by Rey (2003).
During <u>this process</u>, cracks appeared in the
limestone.*

You can refer forward by using 'following'
as an adjective, or 'the following' as a noun
phrase.

*The <u>following</u> passage summarizes
Schmidt's views:...
Symptoms may include any of <u>the following</u>:
chest pains, headaches, difficulty breathing,
and joint pains.*

You can use the adverbs 'above' and 'below' to
refer back and forward to other parts of your
text.

> *The process described <u>above</u> was repeated on three sets of data.*

> *The changes, discussed <u>below</u>, resulted in severe energy shortages.*

Sentence connectors

Sentence connectors show the relationship between two sentences, clauses, or sections of text.

If you want to add another point, you can use 'additionally', 'in addition', 'also', furthermore', or 'moreover'.

> *Previous research has been based on small data samples. <u>Additionally</u>, there have been no interview-based studies.*

If you want to make a contrast, you can use 'conversely', 'however', 'in contrast', 'on the other hand', or 'nevertheless'.

> *Taylor (1994) argues that gender is not a contributing factor. <u>In contrast</u>, Peters (1998) claims that the problem mainly affects women.*

If you want to show the result of something, you can use 'consequently', 'as a result', 'therefore', or 'thus'.

> *There were four groups who were most at risk of unemployment, and <u>therefore</u> most affected by the policies.*

If you want to show the purpose of something, you can use 'in order to' or 'so that'.

> *Several changes are needed <u>in order to</u> improve accuracy.*

Academic style

Being impersonal

In academic writing, it is important to present your text using an impersonal voice. This allows you to focus on the issues rather than on the people involved. The structures below are especially useful for avoiding 'I'.

You can use impersonal 'it' and a passive form of a reporting verb if you are stating an opinion held by an unspecified group of people.

> *<u>It is</u> widely <u>believed</u> that this substance is harmful.*
> *<u>It was acknowledged</u> that resources were unevenly distributed.*

You can put a word such as 'findings' or 'results' in subject position.

> *These <u>findings</u> suggest that there are two different processing methods.*
> *The <u>results</u> show that this problem is widespread.*

You can use the passive without 'by' to describe procedures.

> *The tissue sample <u>was removed</u>, analysed and stored.*

Expressing uncertainty

You can use more cautious language when you think that other people may disagree with your statement, or when you want to express uncertainty about whether or not a statement is true.

You can use modal verbs such as 'can', 'could', 'might', and 'may'.

> *These symptoms <u>may</u> indicate a more severe form of the disease.*

You can use adverbs such as 'possibly', 'arguably', 'apparently', 'normally', and 'typically'.

> *There are, <u>arguably</u>, more efficient methods.*

You can use prepositional phrases such as 'in some respects', 'in some cases', 'in general', and 'in principle'.

> *Current models are inadequate <u>in some respects</u>.*

The grammar of business English

Introduction

This unit describes grammatical patterns that are common in business English. Examples of how language is used are organized into three areas:

- presenting information
- meetings
- negotiating

Presenting information

There are many business situations in which you have to present information, for example in interviews, conferences, reports, and meetings. This section describes some of the most common grammatical forms used in these situations.

Talking about the past, present, and future

In business contexts, it is often necessary to focus on the present. You use the present simple to talk about permanent facts and routines.

> We _offer_ a wide range of services.
> The first thing we _do_ is a site survey.

You use the present progressive to talk about ongoing change.

> *The economy <u>is improving</u>.*
> *We <u>are expanding</u> our range of products.*

Even when you are talking about the past, it is often important to show how past events are relevant now. You can use the present perfect to do this.

> *I <u>have worked</u> in sales for twenty years.*
> *We <u>have made</u> changes based on customer feedback.*

If you want to talk about a completed situation or event in the past, you use the past simple.

> *I successfully <u>completed</u> my degree last year.*

Making predictions is another common feature of business English. You use 'will' or 'be going to' to make predictions.

> *The cuts <u>will</u> have a negative effect on the economy.*
> *Earnings <u>are going to</u> come down sharply.*

If you want to politely make a negative prediction, you can use 'I don't think...' followed by a clause with 'will' or 'be going to'.

> *<u>I don't think</u> this project is going to be a great success.*

You can use the modals 'could', 'may', or 'might' to say that it is possible that something will happen.

> These changes <u>could cause</u> huge problems
> for the rest of Europe.
> New technology <u>might be able to reduce</u> our
> costs.

Making contrasts and comparisons

It is often necessary to compare products,
companies, or situations. You can use
comparative adjectives to do this.

> Software is <u>more profitable than</u> hardware.
> Kondex is <u>bigger than</u> Gartex in terms of
> sales.

You can also use 'not as ... as'.

> Our factories are still <u>not as efficient as</u> the
> car plants in Japan.

You use conjunctions like 'while', 'although',
'in spite of', and 'despite' to make a contrast.

> <u>Although</u> most of their profits are from
> mobile phones, they sell a range of other
> products.
> Sales have increased <u>in spite of</u> the crisis.

Meetings

Business meetings are in some ways like
ordinary conversations: people make
suggestions, ask questions, and interrupt each
other. However, in business contexts, being
persuasive but polite is particularly important.

Making suggestions

You can make suggestions using 'can' and 'could'.

> _Could we_ maybe develop a new payment system?
> _Can we_ ask Network Solutions to help?

To sound more persuasive you can use a negative question.

> _Couldn't we_ ask them to come in for a demonstration?
> _Can't we_ discuss this later?

You can also use 'Let's ...' and 'Why don't we ...' to make suggestions.

> _Let's_ look at a practical example.
> _Why don't we_ move on to the next point on the agenda.

Making requests

You can use 'Can you ...' or 'Could you ...' to ask someone to do something. 'Could' is more polite than 'can'.

> _Can you_ summarize the main points, please?
> _Could you_ explain that again?

The phrase 'Would you mind' following by an '-ing' form is also used to make polite requests.

> _Would you mind going_ back to the previous slide?
> _Would you mind just waiting_ a minute while I answer that?

Conditionals with 'if' can also be used in questions to direct a meeting in a polite way.

> _Would it be all right if_ we go over that again?
> _Do you mind if_ we start with a few introductions, please?

Asking questions

You can use indirect questions beginning with 'Can you tell me...', 'Could you tell me...', or 'Do you know...' in order to ask things politely.

> _Can you tell me_ how complaints are dealt with?
> _Could you tell us_ what it would cost?
> _Do you know_ whether the price includes delivery?

Interrupting

You can use 'can I' and 'could I' to interrupt a meeting politely. 'Could' is more polite than 'can'.

> _Can I_ ask a question here?
> _Could I_ just interrupt for a minute?

Negotiating

When you are making a business deal, you often have to negotiate. It is important to be flexible and diplomatic when you are negotiating, and this section describes some of the grammatical forms you can use.

Being flexible

You can use comparatives to show that you are prepared to negotiate on a particular point.

> *I'm looking for a figure <u>closer</u> to three dollars sixty a unit.*
> *Would you be <u>happier</u> with a fixed rate?*

The modals 'could', 'may', and 'might' are used to say that a particular result or situation is possible.

> *Yes, that <u>might</u> be possible.*
> *I can see that this product <u>could</u> have potential.*

You can use conditionals to discuss possible options.

> *The discount could be bigger <u>if you increased the quantity</u>.*
> *<u>If I drop the price</u>, have we got a deal?*

Being diplomatic

You can use expressions like 'a little', 'a bit', and 'rather' before an adjective, to make a negative message seem less strong.

> *That sounds <u>a little expensive</u>.*
> *Unfortunately, we were <u>rather disappointed</u> with the quality of the last delivery.*

Expressions like 'not very', 'not totally', 'not completely', and 'not entirely' followed by a positive adjective sound more diplomatic than using a negative adjective.

*We aren't totally convinced by the proposal.
I wouldn't be very happy with that
arrangement.*

If you want to disagree with someone, or say
something that they may disagree with, you
can sound more polite by using a reporting
verb such as 'I think...' (or 'I don't think ...') or
'I believe ...' (or 'I don't believe ...').

*I don't believe we agreed on a price.
I think we need to develop a different system.*

Another way to disagree politely is to use an
expression of agreement followed by 'but'.

*I see what you mean but I still don't think it's
possible.
I take your point about the costs but we
could still do it.*

Glossary of grammar terms

abstract noun a noun used to refer to a quality, idea, feeling, or experience, rather than a physical object; EG *size, reason, joy*.
→ See Units 16, 62, 78

active verb phrases such as 'gives', 'took', 'has made', which are used when the subject of the verb is the person or thing doing the action or responsible for it. Compare with **passive**.
→ See Unit 86

adjective a word used to tell you more about a person or thing, such as their appearance, colour, size, or other qualities; EG *...a **pretty blue** dress*.
→ See Units 36–44, 55

adjunct another name for **adverbial**.

adverb a word that gives more information about when, how, where, or in what circumstances something happens; EG *quickly, now*.
→ See Units 25, 44–52, 103

adverbial an adverb, or an adverb phrase, prepositional phrase, or noun phrase which does the same job as an adverb; EG *then, very quickly, in the street, the next day*.
→ See Units 46–54

adverbial of degree an adverbial which indicates the amount or extent of a feeling or quality; EG *She felt **extremely** tired*.
→ See Unit 51

adverbial of duration an adverbial which
indicates how long something continues or
lasts; EG *He lived in London **for six years***.
→ See Unit 50

adverbial of frequency an adverbial which
indicates how often something happens;
EG *She **sometimes** goes to the cinema*.
→ See Unit 49

adverbial of manner an adverbial which
indicates the way in which something
happens or is done; EG *She watched **carefully***.
→ See Unit 47

adverbial of place an adverbial which gives
more information about position or
direction; EG *They are **upstairs**..., Move **closer***.
→ See Unit 52–53

adverbial of probability an adverbial
which gives more information about how
sure you are about something; EG *I realized
I'd **probably** lost it*.
→ See Unit 49

adverbial of time an adverbial which gives
more information about when something
happens; EG *I saw her **yesterday***.
→ See Unit 48

adverb phrase two adverbs used together;
EG *She spoke **very quietly**..., He did not play
well enough to win*.
→ See Unit 46

affirmative a clause or sentence in the
affirmative is one which does not contain a
negative word such as 'not' and which is not

a question.

→ See Units 25, 34–35, 49–50

apostrophe s an ending ('s) added to a noun to indicate possession; EG ...*Harriet's daughter...*, *the professor's husband...*, *the Managing Director's secretary.*

→ See Units 25, 27

article → see **definite article**, **indefinite article**

auxiliary another name for **auxiliary verb**.

auxiliary verb one of the verbs 'be', 'have', and 'do' when they are used with a main verb to make verb forms, negatives, and questions. Some grammars include modals in the group of auxiliary verbs.

→ See Units 3, 5, 7, 9–11, **65**

base form the form of a verb without any endings added to it, which is used in the 'to'-infinitive and for the imperative; EG *walk, go, have, be.* The base form is the form you look up in a dictionary.

→ See Units 3, 80, 87

broad negative an adverb which makes a statement almost negative; EG *I barely knew her.*

→ See Unit 13

cardinal number a number used in counting; EG *one, seven, nineteen.*

→ See Units 2, 14, 28, 31, 35–36

classifying adjective an adjective which is used to identify something as being of a particular type, which does not have a

comparative or superlative form, and which cannot be used with adverbs such as 'very'; EG *Indian, wooden, mental.* Compare with **qualitative adjective**.
→ See Unit 39

clause a group of words containing a verb. See also **main clause** and **subordinate clause**.
→ See Unit 1

collective noun a noun that refers to a group of people or things, which can be used with a singular or plural verb; EG *committee, team, family.*
→ See Unit 15

colour adjective an adjective referring to a colour; EG *red, blue, scarlet.*
→ See Unit 41

common noun a noun which refers to a class of people, objects, substances, or concepts; EG *sailor, computer, glass* Compare with **proper noun**.
→ See Unit 17

comparative an adjective or adverb with '-er' on the end or 'more' in front of it; EG *slower, more important, more carefully.*
→ See Units 43–44

complement a noun phrase or adjective, which comes after a linking verb such as 'be', and gives more information about the subject of the clause; EG *She is a **teacher**..., She is **tired**.*
→ See Units 1–3, 62

complex sentence a sentence consisting of

a main clause and a subordinate clause;
EG *She wasn't thinking very quickly because she was tired.*
→ See Unit 1

compound noun a noun which is formed of two or more words; EG *headache, bus stop, mother-in-law.*
→ See Unit 18

compound sentence a sentence consisting of two or more main clauses linked by a conjunction such as 'and', 'or' or 'but';
EG *They picked her up and took her straight into the house.*
→ See Unit 1

conditional clause a subordinate clause, usually starting with 'if' or 'unless', which is used to talk about possible situations and their results; EG *They would be rich **if they had taken my advice**..., We'll go to the park, **unless it rains**.*
→ See Units 74–75

conjunction a word such as 'and', 'because', or 'nor', that links two clauses, groups, or words.
→ See Units 1, 105, 110

continuous another name for **progressive**.

contrast clause a subordinate clause, usually introduced by 'although' or 'in spite of the fact that', which contrasts with a main clause; EG ***Although I like her,** I find her hard to talk to.*
→ See Unit 107

coordinating conjunction a conjunction

such as 'and', 'but', or 'or', which links two main clauses.

→ See Unit 110

countable noun a noun which has both singular and plural forms; EG *dog/dogs, foot/feet, lemon/lemons*.

→ See Units 14, 29, 31–32, 34–35

count noun another name for **countable noun**.

declarative another name for **affirmative**.

defining relative clause a relative clause which identifies the person or thing that is being talked about; EG *...the lady **who lives next door**..., I wrote down everything **that she said***. Compare with **non-defining relative clause**.

→ See Unit 100

definite article the determiner 'the'.

→ See Units 29–30

delexical verb a common verb such as 'give', 'have', 'make', or 'take', which has very little meaning in itself and is used with a noun as object that describes the action; EG *She **gave** a small cry..., I've just **had** a bath*.

→ See Unit 64

demonstrative one of the words 'this', 'that', these', and 'those'; EG *...**this** woman., ...**that** tree..., **That** looks interesting... **This** is fun*.

→ See Unit 23

descriptive adjective an adjective which describes a person or thing, for example indicating their size, age, shape, or colour, rather than expressing your opinion of that person or thing. Compare with **opinion adjective**.

→ See Unit 37

determiner one of a group of words including 'the', 'a', 'some', and 'my', which are used at the beginning of a noun phrase.

→ See Units 2, 14–15, 28–35

direct object a noun phrase referring to the person or thing affected by an action, in a clause with a verb in the active; EG *She wrote **her name**..., I shut **the windows***.

→ See Units 20, 24, 58–60

direct speech speech reported as if it is the words actually spoken by someone.

→ See Unit 81

ditransitive verb a verb with two objects, such as 'give', 'take', or 'sell'; EG *She **gave** me a kiss*.

→ See Unit 59

'-ed' adjective an adjective which has the same form as the '-ed' participle of a verb; EG ...**boiled** potatoes., ...a **broken** wing.

→ See Unit 40

'-ed' form the form of a regular verb used for the past simple and for the '-ed' participle.

→ See Units 3, 65, 102

'-ed' participle a verb form which is used to form the perfect and the passive. Some '-ed' participles are also used as adjectives; EG *watched, broken*.

→ See Units 3, 65, 78, 102

ellipsis the leaving out of words when they are obvious from the context.

emphasizing adjective an adjective such as 'complete' or 'absolute', which stresses how strongly you feel about something; **EG** *I feel like a* **complete** *idiot.*
→ See Unit 42

emphasizing adverb an adverb such as 'absolutely' or 'utterly', which modifies adjectives that express extreme qualities, such as 'astonishing' and 'wonderful'; **EG** *You were* **absolutely** *wonderful.*
→ See Unit 51

first person → see **person**

future → see **verb form**

gerund another name for the '-ing' participle when it is used as a noun.
→ See Units 77, 79–80

'if'-clause → see **conditional clause**

imperative the form of a verb used when giving orders and commands, which is the same as its base form; **EG** **Come** *here…,* **Take** *two tablets every four hours…,* **Enjoy** *yourself.*
→ See Units **4**, 8, 12, 74

impersonal 'it' 'it' used as an impersonal subject to introduce new information; **EG** **It**'s *raining…,* **It**'s *ten o'clock.*
→ See Units 20–21, 38, 55, 62, 84, 104, 109

indefinite adverb a small group of adverbs including 'anywhere' and 'somewhere' which are used to indicate place in a general way.
→ See Unit 25

indefinite article the determiners 'a' and 'an'.
→ See Unit 31

indefinite pronoun a small group of pronouns including 'someone' and 'anything' which are used to refer to people or things without saying exactly who or what they are.
→ See Units **25**, 102–103

indirect object an object used with verbs that take two objects. For example, in 'I gave him the pen' and 'I gave the pen to him', 'him' is the indirect object and 'pen' is the direct object. Compare with **direct object**.
→ See Units 20, 24, 59

indirect question a question used to ask for information or help; EG *Do you know where Jane is?..., I wonder which hotel it was*.
→ See Unit 9

indirect speech another name for **reported speech**.

infinitive the base form of a verb; EG *I wanted to go..., She helped me dig the garden*. The infinitive is the form you look up in a dictionary.
→ See Units 11, 38, 40, 62, 73, 78, 84–85, 87, 90, 99, 103, 105–106

'-ing' adjective an adjective which has the same form as the '-ing' participle of a verb; EG *...a smiling face., ...a winning streak*.
→ See Unit 40

'-ing' participle a verb form ending in '-ing' which is used to make verb forms, and as an adjective or a noun. Also called the **present participle**.

→ See Units 3, 40, 77, 79–80, 102

interrogative pronoun one of the pronouns 'who', 'whose', 'whom', 'what', and 'which', when they are used to ask questions.
→ See Unit 6

interrogative sentence a sentence in the form of a question.
→ See Unit 5

intransitive verb a verb which does not take an object; EG *She **arrived**..., I **was yawning***. Compare with **transitive verb**.
→ See Unit 58

irregular verb a verb that has three or five forms, or whose forms do not follow the normal rules.
→ See Unit 3 and irregular verb tables

linking verb a verb which takes a complement rather than an object; EG *be, become, seem, appear.*
→ See Unit 62

main clause a clause which does not depend on another clause, and is not part of another clause.
→ See Unit 1

main verb all verbs which are not auxiliaries or modals.
→ See Units 3, 5, 65

manner clause a subordinate clause which describes the way in which something is done, usually introduced with 'as' or 'like'; EG *She talks **like her mother used to***.
→ See Units 76, 108

modal a verb such as 'can', 'might', or 'will', which is always the first word in a verb phrase and is followed by the base form of a verb. Modals are used to express requests, offers, suggestions, wishes, intentions, politeness, possibility, probability, certainty, obligation, and so on.
→ See Units 7–8, 22, 68–69, 72, 75, **87-99**, 105

mood the mood of a clause is the way in which the verb forms are used to show whether the clause is a statement, command, or question.

negative a negative clause, question, sentence, or statement is one which has a negative word such as 'not', and indicates the absence or opposite of something, or is used to say that something is not the case; EG *I don't know you…*, *I'll never forget.* Compare with **positive**.
→ See Units 4, **11-13**, 65, 88

negative word a word such as 'never', 'no', 'not', 'nothing', or 'nowhere', which makes a clause, question, sentence, or statement negative.
→ See Units 3–4, 7–8, 10–**12**, 25, 28, 32, 35, 88

non-defining relative clause a relative clause which gives more information about someone or something, but which is not needed to identify them because we already know who or what they are; EG *That's Mary,* *who was at university with me.* Compare with **defining relative clause**.

→ See Unit 101

non-finite clause a 'to'-infinitive clause, '-ed' clause, or '-ing' clause.

→ See Units 77–80, 102

noun a word which refers to people, things, ideas, feelings, or qualities; EG *woman, Harry, guilt*.

→ See Units 2, **14-19**, 28–36, 56, 64, 102–103

noun phrase a group of words which acts as the subject, complement, or object of a verb, or as the object of a preposition.

→ See Units 1–**2**, 46–48, 52

object a noun phrase which refers to a person or thing that is affected by the action described by a verb or preposition. Compare with **subject**.

→ See Units 20, 24, **58-64**

object pronoun one of a set of pronouns including 'me', 'him', and 'them', which are used as the object of a verb or preposition. Object pronouns are also used as complements after 'be'; EG *I hit **him**..., It's **me***.

→ See Unit 20

opinion adjective an adjective which you use to express your opinion of a person or thing, rather than just describing them. Compare with **descriptive adjective**.

→ See Unit 37

ordinal number a number used to indicate where something comes in an order or sequence; EG *first, fifth, tenth, hundredth*.

participle a word formed from a verb and

used for making different verb forms. Verbs have two participles, an '-ing' participle and an '-ed' participle.

→ See Units 3, 40, 65, 77, 79–80, 102

particle an adverb or preposition which combines with verbs to form phrasal verbs.

→ See Unit 63

passive verb phrases such as 'was given', 'were taken', 'had been made', which are used when the subject of the verb is the person or thing that is affected by the action. Compare with **active**.

→ See Units 78, **86**

past form the form of a verb, often ending in '-ed', which is used for the past simple.

→ See Units 3, 67

past participle → see **'-ed' participle**

past tense → see **verb form**

perfect → see **verb form**

person one of the three classes of people who can be involved in something that is said. The person or people who are speaking or writing are called the first person ('I', 'we'). The person or people who are listening or reading are called the second person ('you'). The person, people or things that are being talked about are called the third person ('he', 'she', 'it', 'they').

personal pronoun one of the group of words including 'I', 'you', and 'me', which are used to refer back to yourself, the people you are talking to, or the people or things you are talking about.

→ See also object pronoun and subject pronoun. See Units **20**, 110

phrasal verb a combination of a verb and a particle, which together have a different meaning to the verb on its own; EG *back down, hand over, look forward to*.

→ See Units 18, **63**, 77

plural the form of a countable noun or verb, which is used to refer to or talk about more than one person or thing; EG *Dogs have ears...*, *The women were outside*.

→ See Units 2, 14–15

plural noun a noun which is normally used only in the plural form; EG *trousers, scissors*.

→ See Unit 15

positive a positive clause, question, sentence, or statement is one which does not contain a negative word such as 'not'. Compare with **negative**.

→ See Units 25, 34–35, 49–50

possessive one of the determiners 'my', 'your', 'his', 'her', 'its', 'our', or 'their', which is used to show that one person or thing belongs to another; EG *...your car*.

→ See Units **27**–28

possessive adjective another name for **possessive**.

possessive pronoun one of the pronouns 'mine', 'yours', 'hers', 'his', 'ours', or 'theirs'.

→ See Units **27**, 45

preposition a word such as 'by', 'with' or

'from', which is always followed by a noun
phrase.
→ See Units 5, 20, 24, **52-57**, 59, 61, 63, 100

prepositional phrase a structure consisting
of a preposition followed by a noun phrase
as its object; EG *on the table, by the sea*.
→ See Units 27, 40, 44, 46-48, 51, 54–57, 105

present participle → see **'-ing' participle**

present tense → see **verb form**

progressive a verb form which contains a
form of the verb 'be' and an '-ing' participle;
EG *She **was laughing**…, They **had been playing**
badminton*. See **verb form**.
→ See Unit 68

pronoun a word which you use instead of a
noun, when you do not need or want to
name someone or something directly;
EG *it, you, none*.
→ See Units 6, **20–21**, 23–27, 45, 100–103, 110

proper noun a noun which is the name of a
particular person, place, organization,
building, or period of time. Proper nouns
are always written with a capital letter;
EG *Nigel, Edinburgh, the United Nations,
Christmas*. Compare with **common noun**
→ See Unit 17

purpose clause a subordinate clause which
is used to talk about the intention that
someone has when they do something;
EG *I came here **in order to ask you out to dinner**.*
→ See Unit 105

qualifier a word or group of words, such

as an adjective, prepositional phrase, or relative clause, which comes after a noun and gives more information about it; EG …*the person **involved**.*, …*a book **with a blue cover**.*, …*the shop **that I went into**.*
→ See Units 27, 100–102

qualitative adjective an adjective which is used to indicate a quality, which has a comparative and superlative form, and which can be used with adverbs such as 'very'; EG *funny, intelligent, small*. Compare with **classifying adjective**.
→ See Unit 39

question a sentence which normally has the verb in front of the subject, and which is used to ask someone about something; EG *Have you any money?*
→ See Units **5–10**, 11, 66, 83, 88

question tag an auxiliary or modal with a pronoun, which is used to turn a statement into a question. EG *He's very friendly, **isn't he**?…, I can come, **can't I**?*
→ See Units 7–8

reason clause a subordinate clause, usually introduced by 'because', 'since', or 'as', which is used to explain why something happens or is done; EG ***Since you're here,*** *we'll start.*
→ See Unit 105

reciprocal verb a verb which describes an action which involves two people doing the same thing to each other; EG *I **met** you at the dance…, We've **met** one another before…,*

They **met** in the street.
→ See Unit 61

reflexive pronoun a pronoun ending in '-self' or '-selves', such as 'myself' or 'themselves', which you use as the object of a verb when you want to say that the object is the same person or thing as the subject of the verb in the same clause; EG He hurt **himself.**
→ See Unit 24

reflexive verb a verb which is normally used with a reflexive pronoun as object; EG He **contented himself** with the thought that he had the only set of keys to the car.
→ See Unit 60

regular verb a verb that has four forms, and follows the normal rules.
→ See Unit 3

relative clause a subordinate clause which gives more information about someone or something mentioned in the main clause. See also **defining relative clause** and **non-defining relative clause**.
→ See Units **100-101**, 103

relative pronoun 'that' or a 'wh'-word such as 'who' or 'which', when it is used to introduce a relative clause; EG ...the girl **who** was carrying the bag.
→ See Units 100–101

reported clause the clause in a reporting structure which indicates what someone has said; EG She said **that I couldn't see her.**

→ See Units 82–85

reported question a question which is
reported using a reporting structure rather
than the exact words used by the speaker.
See also **indirect question**.
→ See Unit 83

reported speech the words you use to
report what someone has said, rather than
using their actual words. Also called
indirect speech.
→ See Units 82–85

reporting clause the clause in a reporting
structure which contains the reporting verb.
→ See Units 82, 84

reporting structure a structure which is
used to report what someone says or
thinks, rather than repeating their exact
words; EG *She told me she'd be late.*
→ See Units 82–85

reporting verb a verb which describes what
people say or think; EG *suggest, say, wonder.*
→ See Units 81-82, 84–85

result clause a subordinate clause
introduced by 'so', 'so...that', or 'such...(that)',
which indicates the result of an action or
situation; EG *I don't think there's any more
news, **so I'll finish.***
→ See Unit 106

second person → see **person**

semi-modal a term used by some
grammars to refer to the verbs 'dare', 'need',
and 'used to', which behave like modals in

some structures.

→ See Units 71, 80, 98

sentence a group of words which express a statement, question, or command. A sentence usually has a verb and a subject, and may be a simple sentence with one clause, or a compound or complex sentence with two or more clauses. In writing, a sentence has a capital letter at the beginning and a full-stop, question mark, or exclamation mark at the end.

→ See Units 1, 74, 100–101, 104–110

short form a form in which one or more letters are omitted and two words are joined together, for example an auxiliary or modal and 'not', or a subject pronoun and an auxiliary or modal; EG *aren't, couldn't, he'd, I'm, it's, she's*.

→ See Unit 11

simple a present or past verb form without an auxiliary verb; EG ...*I wait.*, ...*she sang.* See **verb form**.

→ See Units 66-71, 73

singular the form of a countable noun or verb which is used to refer to or talk about one person or thing; EG *A box was on the table...*, *That woman is my mother*.

→ See Units 14–15

singular noun a noun which is normally used only in the singular form; EG *the sun, a bath*.

→ See Unit 15

subject the noun phrase in a clause that refers to the person or thing who does the action expressed by the verb; **EG** *We were going shopping.* Compare with **object**.
→ See Units 1, 3, 5, 9–10, 14, 16, 20–22, 25, 30, 46, 60, 77–79, 83–85, 88, 110

subject pronoun one of the set of pronouns including 'I', 'she', and 'they', which are used as the subject of a verb.
→ See Unit 20

subordinate clause a clause which must be used with a main clause and is not usually used alone, for example a time clause, conditional clause, relative clause, or result clause, and which begins with a subordinating conjunction such as 'because' or 'while'.
→ See Units 1, 74–76, 100–101, 104–108, 110

subordinating conjunction a conjunction such as 'although', 'as if', 'because' or 'while', which you use to begin a subordinate clause; **EG** *He laughed as if he'd said something funny.*
→ See Unit 110

superlative an adjective or adverb with '-est' on the end or 'most' in front of it; **EG** *thinnest, quickest, most beautiful.*
→ See Units 37, **43-45**, 78

tag question a statement to which a question tag has been added; **EG** *She's quiet, isn't she?..., You've got a car, haven't you?*
→ See Units 7–8

tense the verb form which shows whether you are referring to the past or the present.

'that'-clause a clause starting with 'that', used mainly when reporting what someone has said; EG *She said **that she'd wash up for me.***

→ See Units 38, 40, 84–85, 103

third person → see **person**

time clause a subordinate clause which indicates the time of an event; EG *I'll phone you **when I get back**.*

→ See Unit 104

time expression a noun phrase used as an adverbial of time; EG *last night, the day after tomorrow, the next time.*

→ See Unit 48

'to'-infinitive the base form of a verb preceded by 'to'; EG *to go, to have, to jump.*

→ See Units 11, 38, 40, 62, 73, 78–80, 84–85, 87, 90, 99, 103, 105–106

transitive verb a verb which takes an object; EG *She's **wasting** her money.* Compare with **intransitive verb**.

→ See Unit 58

uncountable noun a noun which has only one form, takes a singular verb, and is not used with 'a' or numbers. Uncountable nouns often refer to substances, qualities, feelings, activities, and abstract ideas; EG *coal, courage, anger, help, fun.*

→ See Units **16**, 29, 32, 34–35

uncount noun another name for

uncountable noun.

verb a word which is used with a subject to say what someone or something does, or what happens to them; EG *sing, spill, die*.
→ See Units 3–4, 10, 57–73, 77–86

verb form the form of a verb which shows whether you are referring to the past, present, or future, and whether you are indicating completeness or continuation.
→ See Units 65–73

future 'will' or 'shall' with the base form of the verb, used to refer to future events; EG *She* **will come** *tomorrow...,* **I shall** *ask her as soon as I see her.*
→ See Unit 72

future perfect 'will' or 'shall' with 'have' and an '-ed' participle, used to refer to future events; EG *I* **shall have finished** *by tomorrow.*
→ See Units 69, 72

future perfect progressive 'will' or 'shall' with 'have been' and an '-ing' participle, used to refer to future events; EG *I* **will have been walking** *for three hours by then.*
→ See Units 68–69, 72

future progressive 'will' or 'shall' with 'be' and an '-ing' participle, used to refer to future events; EG *She* **will be going** *soon.*
→ See Units 68, 72

past perfect 'had' with an '-ed' participle, used to refer to past events; EG *She* **had finished** *her meal.*

→ See Units 67, 69, 71

past perfect progressive 'had been' with an '-ing' participle, used to refer to past events; EG *He **had been waiting** for hours.*

→ See Units 67–69, 71

past progressive 'was' or 'were' with an '-ing' participle, usually used to refer to past events; EG *They **were worrying** about it all day yesterday.*

→ See Units 67–68, 71

past simple the past form of a verb, used to refer to past events; EG *They **waited**.*

→ See Units 67, 71, 82

present perfect 'have' or 'has' with an '-ed' participle, used to refer to past events which exist in the present; EG *She **has loved** him for over ten years.*

→ See Units 66, 69, 71, 73

present perfect progressive 'have been' or 'has been' with an '-ing' participle, used to refer to past events which continue in the present; EG *We **have been sitting** here for hours.*

→ See Units 66, 68–69, 71

present progressive the present simple of 'be' with an '-ing' participle, usually used to refer to present events; EG *Things **are improving**..., She **is working**.*

→ See Units 66, 68, 70, 73

present simple the base form and the third person singular form of a verb, usually used to refer to present events; EG *I **like***

bananas..., My sister **hates** them.

→ See Units 66, 68, 73, 82

verb phrase a main verb, or a main verb
with one or more auxiliaries, a modal, or a
modal and an auxiliary, which is used with
a subject to say what someone does, or
what happens to them; EG I'll **show** them...,
She's **been** sick.

→ See Units 1, **3**, 5, 11–12, 65, 87

'wh'-question a question which expects the
answer to give more information than just
'yes' or 'no'; EG What happened next?..., Where
did he go? Compare with **'yes/no'-question**.

→ See Units 5–**6**, 9, 83

'wh'-word one of a group of words starting
with 'wh-', such as 'what', 'when', or 'who',
which are used in 'wh'-questions. 'How' is
also called a 'wh'-word because it behaves
like the other 'wh'-words.

→ See Units 5–**6**, 78, 83, 85, 100–101

'yes/no'-question a question which can be
answered by just 'yes' or 'no', without giving
any more information; EG Would you like
some more tea? Compare with **'wh'-
question**.

→ See Units 5, 7, 10, 83

Irregular verbs

INFINITIVE	PAST TENSE	-ed PARTICIPLE
arise	arose	arisen
awake	awoke	awoken
be *(am, are, is)*	was, were	been
bear	bore	born(e)
beat	beat	beaten
become	became	become
begin	began	begun
bend	bent	bent
bet	bet	bet
bind	bound	bound
bite	bit	bitten
bleed	bled	bled
blow	blew	blown
break	broke	broken
breed	bred	bred
bring	brought	brought
build	built	built
burn	burnt, burned	burnt, burned
burst	burst	burst
buy	bought	bought
cast	cast	cast
catch	caught	caught
choose	chose	chosen
cling	clung	clung
come	came	come
cost	cost	cost
creep	crept	crept
cut	cut	cut

INFINITIVE	PAST TENSE	-ed PARTICIPLE
deal	dealt	dealt
dig	dug	dug
do (*does*)	did	done
draw	drew	drawn
dream	dreamed, dreamt	dreamed, dreamt
drink	drank	drunk
drive	drove	driven
eat	ate	eaten
fall	fell	fallen
feed	fed	fed
feel	felt	felt
fight	fought	fought
find	found	found
fling	flung	flung
fly	flew	flown
forbid	forbade	forbidden
forecast	forecast	forecast
forget	forgot	forgotten
forgive	forgave	forgiven
freeze	froze	frozen
get	got	got (*US*) gotten
give	gave	given
go (*goes*)	went	gone
grind	ground	ground
grow	grew	grown
hang	hung	hung
hang (= *execute*)	hanged	hanged
have (*has*)	had	had

INFINITIVE	PAST TENSE	-ed PARTICIPLE
hear	heard	heard
hide	hid	hidden
hit	hit	hit
hold	held	held
hurt	hurt	hurt
keep	kept	kept
kneel	knelt, kneeled	knelt, kneeled
know	knew	known
lay	laid	laid
lead	led	led
lean	leant, leaned	leant, leaned
leap	leapt, leaped	leapt, leaped
learn	learnt, learned	learnt, learned
leave	left	left
lend	lent	lent
let	let	let
lie	lay	lain
lie (= say something untrue)	lied	lied
light	lit, lighted	lit, lighted
lose	lost	lost
make	made	made
mean	meant	meant
meet	met	met
mistake	mistook	mistaken

INFINITIVE	PAST TENSE	-ed PARTICIPLE
mow	mowed	mown, mowed
pay	paid	paid
put	put	put
quit	quit	quit
read	read	read
ride	rode	ridden
ring	rang	rung
rise	rose	risen
run	ran	run
saw	sawed	sawn
say	said	said
see	saw	seen
seek	sought	sought
sell	sold	sold
send	sent	sent
set	set	set
sew	sewed	sewn
shake	shook	shaken
shear	sheared	shorn, sheared
shed	shed	shed
shine	shone	shone
shoot	shot	shot
show	showed	shown
shrink	shrank	shrunk
shut	shut	shut
sing	sang	sung
sink	sank	sunk
sit	sat	sat

INFINITIVE	PAST TENSE	-ed PARTICIPLE
sleep	slept	slept
slide	slid	slid
sling	slung	slung
slit	slit	slit
smell	smelt, smelled	smelt, smelled
sow	sowed	sown
speak	spoke	spoken
speed	sped, speeded	sped, speeded
spell	spelt, spelled	spelt, spelled
spend	spent	spent
spill	spilt, spilled	spilt, spilled
spin	spun	spun
spit	spat	spat
spoil	spoiled, spoilt	spoiled, spoilt
spread	spread	spread
spring	sprang	sprung
stand	stood	stood
steal	stole	stolen
stick	stuck	stuck
sting	stung	stung
stink	stank	stunk
stride	strode	stridden
strike	struck	struck
swear	swore	sworn
sweep	swept	swept

INFINITIVE	PAST TENSE	-ed PARTICIPLE
swell	swelled	swollen, swelled
swim	swam	swum
swing	swung	swung
take	took	taken
teach	taught	taught
tear	tore	torn
tell	told	told
think	thought	thought
throw	threw	thrown
thrust	thrust	thrust
tread	trod	trodden
wake	woke, waked	woken, waked
wear	wore	worn
weave	wove	woven
weep	wept	wept
win	won	won
wind	wound	wound
wring	wrung	wrung
write	wrote	written